# A Victorian Childhood

## RECOLLECTIONS and REFLECTIONS

### WALTER LITTLER

HORSESHOE PUBLICATIONS . WARRINGTON . CHESHIRE

First published in Great Britain in 1997 by Marion Seymour,

First Reprint 1998

ISBN 1.899310.35.5

This edition published 1998 by
HORSESHOE PUBLICATIONS
Box 37, Kingsley, Warrington,
Cheshire WA6 8DR

Printed and bound in Great Britain by
DELMAR PRESS LTD
Nantwich, Cheshire

*This book is posthumously dedicated to the author's family
and especially to the younger members
who have taken such an interest in it.*

## ACKNOWLEDGEMENT

We wish to express our gratitude and thanks to Ralph Seymour, grandson, son and nephew, without whose enthusiasm, resourcefulness and hard work the original edition of this book would never have been published.

*The Author*

# EXPLANATORY NOTE

The unit of currency during Walter Littler's life, and for a decade after his death, was based on the Imperial system.

The basic unit then, as now, was the pound sterling, but it was divided into twenty shillings, and these were further divided into twelve pennies (£.s.d.). Each penny was divided into two half pennies (ha'pennies) and four farthings. Thus the modern penny is equivalent to 2.4 old pennies.

The coinage was divided into three series: Gold (Sovereign and half Sovereign), Bronze (penny, ha'penny, and farthing), and Silver for the remainder. The coins in each group were in proportion by weight, thus the value of a mixed bag of silver could be determined by simple weighing. This was an advantage when paying in money at the bank, but produced a very wide range of weights in the individual coins. Thus the silver half Crown was ten times the weight of the threepenny-bit, which was much smaller than the present 5p coin (relevant to one of Walter's stories). The Crown was too heavy for general use, and restricted to special issues.

Currency notes did not appear in common circulation until the First World War, although some banks introduced them much earlier.

The use of the suffix 'P' in modern usage e.g. 8P arose from the necessity to distinguish between old and new. Previous usage would have been to speak of eightpence (8d). The sixpenny piece was commonly called a 'tanner', and the shilling was known as a 'bob'. Thus eight shillings (8/-) would normally be spoken of as 'eight bob'. Combinations of values were abbreviated in speech, thus one shilling and sixpence (1/6) would become 'one and six', and one pound one shilling and sixpence (£1 1s 6d) would become 'one pound one and six'.

It was common for professional fees to be charged in guineas (£1-1/-), though no such coin was in use at that time.

The coinage of the realm in the 1890's was as follows:

|                | Imperial            | Decimal Equivalent |
|----------------|---------------------|--------------------|
| Sovereign      | £1                  | £1                 |
| Half Sovereign | 10 shillings (10/-) | 50p                |
| Crown          | 5 shillings (5/-)   | 25p                |
| Half Crown     | 2/6                 | 12.5p              |
| Florin         | 2 shillings (2/-)   | 10p                |

| Shilling | (1/-) | 5p |
| Sixpence | (6d) | 2.5p |
| Threepence | (3d) | 1.25p |
| Penny | (1d) | 0.42p |
| Ha'penny | (½d) | 0.21p |
| Farthing | (¼d) | 0.1p |

Inflation scarcely existed in the latter part of the nineteenth century - hackney-carriage fares were displayed in cast iron by some licensing authorities - but all that was to change during the present century. Thus it was necessary to earn £12-50 in 1959 to maintain the spending power that £1 had in 1890, and this increased to £49 by 1997.

# FOREWORD

The author intended this little book as a legacy to us, his two daughters, and especially to his grandchildren. Born in 1883, he completed the manuscript in 1959, but died the following year before he was able to make a serious attempt at getting it published. It has lain fallow ever since.

The most self-effacing of men, it only emerges from incidental references even that he trained as a teacher, much less that he won one of the 'handful of scholarships' he refers to. In fact he was well-known in the academic world, and there must be many still alive to whom his name will be familiar.

He was Senior Science Master at Hele's School, Exeter, for almost forty years, and in the late 'twenties he started writing a series of chemistry and physics text books. At the height of their success, one or more of them was in use in a third of the schools in this country catering for School Certificate, and they also had substantial overseas sales. They continued as best-sellers until his death in 1960, after which of course they could no longer be kept up-to-date.

When considering the possibility of publication, it has always been seen as a problem that it is a 'then and now' book, with the 'now' element getting ever more out-of-date. However, it is now *so* out-of-date that the contrast between 1997 and 1959 is of interest in its own right. Such has been the ever-increasing pace of change fuelled by scientific advances and the revolution in social attitudes, it could be argued that more divides us from 1959 than divided him from 1890, despite the two World Wars which dominated the first half of the century.

He was the youngest but two of a large Victorian family. His parents had both turned forty when he was born, and their recollections, which crop up frequently in the book, go back a hundred and fifty years.

In 1909 he married his boyhood sweetheart, Annie Holt. The Holts were a well-known Runcorn family with a Methodist pedigree going well back into the eighteenth century. There are several references to them in the book.

The book is basically as he wrote it, but oddly enough he left out a number of the funny stories we remember him telling us as children, so many of these have been included. All additions are matters of fact. No opinion is expressed which was not his own.

In conclusion, one could say of him that he was a deep and original thinker, and no-one could have come nearer to living the Christian ethic.

He had a very keen sense of humour which enlivens the whole book, and as every good Christian should be, he was an unquenchable optimist.

Even had he lived to see the grievous state that our society is in today, he would have identified good things in it, notably the brighter prospects for world peace, and been as convinced as ever that this is no more than one of the inevitable setbacks on the long march to a better world and a better life for all.

He wrote a preface, and about the book in general we cannot do better than quote it verbatim.

*Marion and Winifred 1997*

# FOREWORD TO THE NEW EDITION

The original hard-back edition of 'A Victorian Childhood' proved so popular that it has been decided to reissue it in 'soft-back'.

There are minor changes, in particular the insertion of the Epilogue with which the book concludes. It was emphasised in Walter's preface that the book was intended primarily as a social history, illustrated by events recalled from his own young life and the life of the family into which he was born. Information outside and beyond that period would have seemed irrelevant to him, but so many readers of the original publication have been left disappointed at not knowing 'what happened to them all' that it has been decided to round off the family history in true Victorian style.

Apart from this there are a few factual corrections and small amendments to the text, which are largely the result of comments from interested readers. In addition, several passages and anecdotes omitted from the original publication have been included.

Walter's elder daughter Winifred, who co-operated enthusiastically in the project has now sadly died, but she did live just long enough to see the first edition in print.

Since her death a number of old photographs have come to light which have made it possible to provide some further topical illustrations for the new edition.

*Marion Seymour 1998*

# PREFACE

Any adult person today, especially if he is rather more than middle-aged, must often reflect on the changes that have taken place in his lifetime. The most obvious ones are the material ones, such as the coming of the aeroplane and the increased use of motor vehicles; the radio and television sets in every home; the development of atomic energy which may provide man with an unlimited supply of power, but on the other hand involve him in total destruction.

Less obvious but no less important are man's changes in thought, especially as regards religion and his place in society; changes in fact in his ideas of his relationship to God on the one hand and his fellow-men on the other.

So I have tried to recall the social and material conditions of life some sixty years ago together with what I may call the atmosphere of religious thought at the time.

At first glance the picture might seem to be only a very partial one, for the scene seldom strays far from Runcorn, a small industrial town on the Cheshire side of the Mersey, while the religious atmosphere of the home I describe, though it might be found in thousands of others, was by no means universal. It is probable however that material and social conditions in Runcorn were fairly representative of those existing in England generally, at any rate in industrial England.

In particular, my account of the education provided in a Runcorn elementary school would I think be typical of most elementary schools of the period, while the comparison of past and present, attempted in the last two chapters, is also of general application.

The picture I describe is the picture I saw. It is subjective as well as objective, and that will perhaps give it a special value which would not be found in a coldly objective description, or in statistics. The subjective approach often involves incidents in which I was personally concerned and so to a certain extent the book becomes an autobiography, but only incidentally, and in any case, apart from a few odd references, it relates only to the age period of four to thirteen.

In general the names of persons mentioned are the actual ones, but when on occasion truth has compelled me to be less than complimentary I have given a fictitious name which I have tried to make as obvious as possible. In most cases the person is no longer living, but I have no wish to give pain to relatives who may still be alive.

*W.L. 1959*

# LIST OF ILLUSTRATIONS

**Mother, aged 18**
*This photo was taken in 1862, before she moved to Runcorn*

# CHAPTER 1

# My Mother

I have already said that this little book is not first and foremost an autobiography. It does, however, contain a good deal of material relating to the first ten or twelve years of my life, and so I will follow well-established precedent by giving some account of my family history. In this respect my task will be a very simple one, because I know almost nothing of my forebears further back than my grandparents, and very little about them.

My grandparents on my mother's side lived at Margate, in Kent. My grandfather was a building contractor in a small way of business and the family lived in moderate comfort. But on a dark windy night - it was Christmas Eve of 1848 - my grandmother was very worried that he had not returned home though it was long after his usual time. The following morning his body was found at the foot of the cliffs. Apparently he had missed his way in the dark and been blown over.

There were four children and my mother, born in 1844, was the youngest but one. There was not much money, and the poor widow didn't make the best use of what there was because she took to drink. She did her drinking in private so it was quite 'respectable', but it took money that was needed for necessities. Sometimes the children were short of food. I have heard my mother describe how she was out walking one day with her still younger brother Walter when they found a small turnip by the roadside, and they were so hungry that they ate it greedily.

In such circumstances one can readily understand that my grandmother was glad enough to let the children shift for themselves as soon as they could. So at the age of nine my mother was acting as general help to a kindly old lady, receiving sixpence a week and full board and lodging. Somehow she had learnt to read and write. As so often in those days, her main reading was the Bible, a book she loved and read to the end of a long life.

I have often heard her speak of service (I think as assistant cook) at a boarding school for Jewish boys. This would certainly be at a later time than the 'sixpence a week' days, and I imagine she would be twelve or thirteen. At this school much importance was attached to a knowledge of the Old Testament, and she often related with a chuckle that when a boy was unable to answer a question in Scripture, the teacher would say "We'd better send for Sarah, *she'll* know" - and sure enough she did! She also discovered that by indulging in the reprehensible habit of listening at keyholes when she happened to be near a classroom, she could acquire scraps of knowledge - free.

She had been brought up Church of England but came under Wesleyan influence while still a young girl. John Wesley had by this time been dead for nearly seventy years, but the revival which he initiated was far from having spent its force. Indeed, it is difficult for us in these days to realise the soul-shaking effect of some of the religious meetings of the mid-nineteenth century. The threat of eternal punishment for unbelievers had never been a characteristic of Wesley's own preaching, but many who followed him saw hell as a literal, unquenchable fire, and so represented it to the utter terror of their congregations. In my own young days I have heard people describe the agonising experience of being 'under conviction' of sin. It could drive men mad, and sometimes did. Usually however, after days of gloom and terror, and helped by kindly pastors and class leaders, they accepted such assurances as 'thy sins which are many are all forgiven', and the peace which followed was indescribable. I have discussed this point at some length because it was an experience which befell both my parents, with profound effect upon their later lives.

I have before me as I write my mother's first class ticket. The date is within two days of her nineteenth birthday and suggests that she had quite recently passed through the experience of conversion which I have briefly described.

Conversion could, and did, bring about completely changed lives, but it was also associated on occasion with the most contemptible hypocrisy, and just at the moment of attaining her own great spiritual happiness and peace, mother was to learn something of this at first hand.

At the time of which I am speaking, when she was about nineteen, she was in service as cook to the Sandford family. Mr Sandford had a good retail drapery business, and moved from Margate to Runcorn in 1864 or thereabouts, continuing in the same line of trade. He must have found mother a good servant, because he persuaded her to move with the family. There were two other servants besides herself, one of whom worked in the shop.

I remember some of the stories she told me when I was a child. Very strange stories, when one remembers that Mr Sandford was a very religious man and a Wesleyan local preacher. His beliefs forbade that any but the most essential work should be done on the Sabbath, but the Sabbath ended at midnight, so it was obviously quite in order to call the servants at 12. 05 am. Monday was a particularly busy day with the week's washing added to the usual daily round, so one could hardly make too prompt a start. No doubt the girls went to bed as early as possible in the evening, but that would not be until they had cleared up after Sunday supper.

Then there was that little matter of the potatoes. With the one exception of potatoes, which were extremely cheap, Mr and Mrs Sandford kept all food locked up. Mother as cook had to ask Mrs Sandford for all the supplies she needed, but her mistress never produced the least surplus. The servants couldn't have had enough to eat, for they often asked mother whether she could manage to procure some extra for supper. All she could offer was potatoes baked in their jackets, but they were thankful enough for those.

One night she had just taken the potatoes out of the oven when the bell sounded for evening prayers, an established custom in that religious household. Punctuality was insisted upon so she quickly rolled them up in her apron and went into the drawing room. Alas! in the act of opening the door she lost her grip on the apron, and five or six incriminating potatoes rolled out onto the floor.

Mr Sandford both heard and saw, but said nothing. He read a passage from the Bible as usual, and then the little household knelt down, Mr Sandford leading them in extempore prayer. Mother could not remember the first part of the prayer, but never forgot a passage which came a little later: "And, oh Lord, should there be anybody here who has yielded to temptation and purloined her master's goods, may she repent of her sin and obtain Thy forgiveness. " My mother had a very tender conscience, but I don't think she ever repented of trying to give those hungry servants a little extra food!

Another of her stories related to rats. She had several times seen them scuttling about in the cellar and she thought her employer ought to know about it. She mentioned it to him and he was obviously very worried. "Sarah," he said, "I want them got rid of, and I'm going to make you a very generous offer. For every dead rat you can bring me, I'm going to give you fourpence. "

In those days fourpence was a lot of money to anybody as short of it as mother was, but how to earn it! Mother was no fonder of approaching a rat than anybody else would be, but there was that fourpence! Perhaps a whole string of fourpences. . .

The answer to the problem was a broom, which she wielded with such skill and vigour that she had soon killed her first rat, and brought it to Mr Sandford. "Splendid, Sarah, splendid," he said "I'll make a note of it. Fourpence due to you," and he jotted something down in his notebook.

Flushed with success, mother entered with great zest into the rat killing campaign and soon became a real expert. Corpse after corpse was brought to Mr Sandford's notice who never failed to 'make a note of it'. At length she ventured timidly to ask if he would pay her the accumulated fourpences and he made some excuse or other. Several times at intervals she raised the matter until it became quite obvious that he didn't mean to pay. She never received a single penny.

It may seem strange to the modern mind that servants were willing to work in a house where the labours of washing day began just after midnight, and where they didn't get enough to eat. The answer is that towns such as Runcorn had a relatively large working-class population, and for the young woman of those days there was hardly any other occupation than 'service'. If she was dissatisfied with her job, there were plenty of others who were willing to take her place.

And my mother's reaction? As she had been willing to accompany the Sandford family from Kent to Cheshire, it must have seemed nothing unusual to her that the servants were expected to start work immediately after midnight, or that her employer kept a tight hand over the contents of the larder, because presumably this had been his practice in Kent. His meanness and dishonesty over the rat money was another matter.

No doubt she was indignant at the time, but the incident evidently left no permanent bitterness because when in later days she recalled it, she was evidently more impressed by a certain humour in the situation than by any other feeling.

All that I have so far written about my mother is derived from what she told me or the other children about her early life, up to the time that she was twenty or twenty one. I will now try to describe her as I knew her.

It will be obvious from what I have already said that her life had a strong religious basis. Like most religious people of her day she was a 'Fundamentalist', believing that whatever was written in the Bible was true. If you asked her how a God of Love could allow such happenings as, for example, the slaughter of the Amalekites, man, woman and child, she would just say that there are many things in the Bible that we cannot understand, but which will be explained to us some day. 'What I do though knowest not now, but thou shalt know hereafter'.

Bible stories were a regular feature of the bedtime half hour, after we had said our prayers and been tucked up for the night. They were not invariable, for the little anecdotes like the ones of Mr Sandford nearly all came my way at this time. Still, Bible stories were the rule, taken more often from the Old Testament than the New, or perhaps it is that the former made a stronger impression.

I remember that the 'Joseph' stories formed a series lasting several nights, though I found many years later that when the record was concerned with that brazen madam Potiphar's wife, it had been suitably edited.

At other times we stood on Mount Carmel, where we saw an altar with a king and eight hundred and fifty prophets of Baal on the one side, while on the other was Elijah standing alone and concluding his address to the people with the ringing challenge 'and the God who answereth with fire, let him be God'. Then too there was that feast where a drunken king and his nobles are watching the fingers of a man's hand tracing some strange characters on a wall - 'weighed in the balance and found wanting'.

These stories and many another. No wonder we looked forward to them as now, near the end of the day, those of us who are still left look back upon them. Surely these old Bible stories form a rich heritage into which every child should be allowed to enter, for they show as perhaps nothing else can, the poetic and dramatic power of a spiritually great people, still fighting valiantly as they were fighting forty centuries ago for the right to survive.

My mother was a great reader. Nothing very highbrow, but she enjoyed such books as Charlotte Brontë's 'Jane Eyre' and 'The Mill on the Floss'. She also read George McDonald's 'Malcolm' and 'The Marquis of Lossie', and rather surprisingly the Scottish dialect in which they are written did not bother her very much.

But the clear spring to which she always returned was the Bible. Here without question the Book of Psalms was first favourite, but she was also very fond of Proverbs and Ecclesiastes, of Job and parts of Isaiah. Looking back, I realise that she had a strong but uncultivated taste for the poetic, and it found expression in these particular parts of the Bible.

She had an odd way of mixing up her reading with her work. While she was making a bed for instance, her Bible would be open on top of a chest of drawers and while her hands were smoothing out a sheet or plumping up a pillow, she was in thought accompanying Naomi and Ruth as they journeyed from the Moabite country to Bethlehem, or perhaps observing a small man climbing a sycamore tree in order to get a better view of Jesus.

In a good sense of the word she led a double life; active and efficient in carrying out her daily duties and yet, deep down, living a detached spiritual life. The result was a marked serenity amidst a certain hubbub (we were a large family) which would have driven many a woman distracted. All this is not to say that she did not appreciate physical peace and quiet on the rare occasions when they came her way for I have often heard her quote, a little wistfully, that strange passage in Revelations: 'There was silence in the Heaven for the space of half an hour'. To her, there must have been many a time when half an hour's silence would have been heaven indeed!

Until I retired in 1945, my whole working life was spent in teaching, so I have often considered how far my mother's methods with her children conformed to those of a good teacher.

A point greatly and rightly insisted upon in a teacher's training course is that he must first secure the obedience of his class. Mother certainly secured that of hers, and began to take the necessary steps almost from the time that each child was born.

She could have known nothing of modern theories of the subconscious mind, but she seemed to understand instinctively what modern psychology teaches, that to 'give in' to a child, even in the early weeks of life, is merely to store up trouble for the future. In this she may have taken Susannah Wesley for a model. Susannah was the mother of the famous John and Charles, and records that all her children had learnt to 'cry quietly' by the time they were twelve months old. As there were seventeen other young Wesleys, the advantages of this early discipline are obvious!

This insistence on obedience had one immediate benefit for a large family; it served as a great physical safeguard. For instance I can remember many occasions when I and my brother William, who was three and half years older, were in the company of boys who were all bathing in a 'pit'. This was the local name for a deep pond, which may have been of natural formation but was more often one of the flooded workings commonly found in industrial areas. Much as we would have liked to join them, we never thought of doing so. Bathing in pits had very wisely been forbidden, and that decided it. In this way we were able to enjoy the maximum of freedom which is so essential to a child's all-round development, and with it the minimum of risk.

This is not the only benefit derived by the child who has understood that the parental 'No' really means 'No'. Later in life he will often meet with 'No', not from his parents but from the circumstances of life. The rebellious person will be like a caged bird beating its wings against the bars. He will feel frustrated, suffer deeply and become embittered. The one who has learnt to understand 'No' will accept the situation philosophically without a fruitless expenditure of energy and temper. I am not advocating mere passivity and cowardly acquiescence, but when one is sure that a particular path is blocked it is far better to accept the situation and acceptance comes more easily to the man who has learnt the habit early.

It is another great principle of modern teaching methods that promises and threats must not be made without deliberate thought, but having once been made they must be carried out.

This principle too was vigorously applied. How well I remember having saved elevenpence halfpenny, which at a wage of a halfpenny a week had taken quite some doing! Small children are seldom secretive, and the whole household was getting very tired of the information that when Saturday came I should have saved a whole shilling.

But a day or two before I was guilty of some misdemeanour - I do not now remember what it was. Mother knew how to hit where it would hurt, and she said that there would be no halfpenny on Saturday. I didn't say much about it, because I simply could not believe in the possibility of such a calamity. Somehow, when Saturday came it would be alright. But of course, it wasn't! I might have known that protests would be useless but I wept, I shouted, I lay on the carpet and kicked. "It's not a bit of good," mother said. "I said you should not have that halfpenny and that's the end of it. " My lively protests continued for about two hours, and then I gave in. Knowing how tender hearted she was, I realise what it must have cost her to make the threat effective.

She was just as faithful in keeping a promise. About Christmas time of 1897 when I was nearly fifteen, I came to her with a rather hair-brained scheme for a long walking tour in the following summer. I knew an almost insurmountable obstacle would be the cost, for there were no Youth Hostels in those days. My idea was to buy quarter-pound packets of Brook Bond's tea wholesale, from Bates' Grocer's shop in Bridge Street, sell them in the course of my walk and pay the expenses with the profits.

I suppose she thought the scheme so ridiculous that it would never come off and so she agreed to it, probably at a moment when her attention was half distracted by something else. August came and I reminded her of her promise. "I don't remember saying any such thing!" she said. This looked awkward. Luckily though my sister Bessie was able to say "Yes you did, mother. I happened to be there at the time and you did promise him. " "Well if I promised I suppose I must let you go," she said, "but all the same I wish I hadn't. " I ought to have released her from her promise, but at fifteen thoughtfulness for others is seldom a strong feature so I went on my tour, subject only to the very mild condition that I should send her a postcard every evening.

I wish I could report that this Napoleonic scheme worked out as planned in all its details, but financially it was a disaster. I bought twenty two pounds of tea from Mr Bates, intending to renew my stock from time to time as I ran out. I never sold even the twenty two pounds, for I brought four pounds back. The gross cost of the holiday was fifteen shillings and the tea profits were four and sixpence, so I ended up with a debit balance of ten and six.

I started out every morning on a good breakfast, but to keep costs down I lived chiefly for the rest of the day on a mixture of Quaker Oats and sugar. Of my ten days, I spent two poking around Matlock which was my farthest point, and the remaining eight in walking a hundred and thirty two miles, carrying that wretched tea in a canvas portmanteau. I hadn't even a rucksack! Yet I thoroughly enjoyed the experience, and after more than sixty years I still recall it with pleasure.

This was a case in which mother's faithfulness to a principle worked to my advantage, but viewed in retrospect I now feel that her attitude was too unbending. There were occasions when a particular threat or promise ought not to have been made, and in that case she should have said so and withdrawn it, instead of putting herself in the position of having to maintain her stand at all costs.

She was very tactful in her dealings with the neighbours, and often quoted that dictum of Solomon's, 'A soft answer turneth away wrath'. This was well illustrated in the little matter of the captured ball. I should explain that our back gate opened on to Bentinck Street, and almost opposite lived old Mrs Ellison. She sold milk and a few sweets and groceries, making it necessary to keep her front door open so that customers could enter.

One day I was out playing with a ball when unluckily it went right through this open doorway and into her lobby. I realised the critical nature of the situation, but before I could do anything about it she had bounced out of her kitchen and impounded the ball. I asked very politely for its return but was met with a blank refusal. She said she was tired of having children playing round her front door and perhaps this would teach me.

Here was a pretty kettle of fish! That ball had cost threepence: three whole week's wages. (By this time, aged nine, I had been promoted to the penny-a-week rate). Something must be done! I retired to think about it and had soon formulated a brilliant plan. Just inside the door, probably helping to keep it open, there was a mat. It wouldn't be very hard to secure that mat, and then maybe an exchange of booty could be arranged. Moving quickly I obtained the article in question, slipped through our backyard gate, bolted it, and easily climbed to the top of the coal-house which adjoined the gate. Then I called, "Mrs Ellison!"

At first she didn't hear me, but I raised my voice and after two or three more of my efforts she came to the door. Curiously, she didn't notice at this stage that the mat was missing. "Your doormat's gone Mrs Ellison and I've got it," I said. A glance first downwards, and then at me holding up the missing mat, quickly convinced her that the facts were as stated. "I don't want your doormat Mrs Ellison," I continued. "It's no use to me at all. But I do want my ball back, and if you'll let me have it, you shall have your doormat."

"You young thief! You rascal! You good-for-nothing!" she screamed shaking her fist at me. "I'm coming to see your mother about it this very instant!" She came across and started thumping at the bolted gate. "Unfasten the gate this minute!" she shouted. I thought it best to comply, but first hid the mat in the coal-house, then I nipped quickly into the house. I had no wish to be made a prisoner by Mrs Ellison.

She knocked at the door and mother opened it. A moment later the infuriated lady, ignoring the trifling incident of the impounded ball, was telling her that I had stolen her doormat, and unless it was returned at once she would call the police.

"But I can't think he would steal your mat," she said. "The lad isn't a thief, and anyway what would he want a doormat *for*?" I was hovering only a yard or two away. "Come here Walter, and tell me what it's all about."

I told my story, and at the end of it mother was quiet for a moment. Then she said, "I can quite understand how you feel, Mrs Ellison. I know how annoying it can be when children are romping and shouting near one's door, and I expect you felt thoroughly put out, but of course the lad would be nearly heartbroken at the loss of his ball. I'm sure if you could let him off just this once. . ." As the soft answer proceeded I could see Mrs Ellison's wrath gradually being turned away, and she finally agreed to a mutual exchange of property. Yes, mother certainly had tact. Needless to say, when playing ball afterwards I took good care to keep well away from that ever-open door. One can't be too careful with valuable possessions.

I hope in emphasising the strongly religious element in my mother's nature, I have not conveyed the impression that she was forbidding. Far from it! She had a keen sense of humour, which if not very subtle was certainly very lively. She was by nature optimistic and cheerful, and so found it easy to obey such injunctions as 'Be of good cheer' and 'Rejoice evermore'.

She was certainly much given to quoting the scriptures, and I would say the passage she quoted more often than any other was 'The lines have fallen unto me in pleasant places. Yea, I have a goodly heritage'. Anybody whose abiding experience is expressed in such words as these, can hardly help radiating cheerfulness.

*Father*

# CHAPTER 2

# My Father

My father was born in 1841 in the little village of Elton, near Ince, and about ten miles on the Runcorn side of Chester. His mother died when he was three or four years old, and he was only about seven when his father also met with an untimely end. He was found one cold winter's morning, dead in a field. He had probably had too much to drink at the village ale house, and on his way home had lain down and settled into a drunken sleep. The cold had done the rest.

Many years ago, one of my father's elder sisters told me most of the little I know of this grandfather. He was strong and very broad shouldered, ('as broad as he was long' to quote my aunt's description), and I have already indicated that he was no pioneer of the teetotal movement. He was one of those men who when they are in drink are very bad tempered, and this condition was often reached when he had finished work on a Saturday. When he finally arrived home, he would sit down and survey the dinner table. All being well, he would get on morosely with his meal, but it was just about even chances that he would be dissatisfied with the food provided, in which case it was his disconcerting habit to sweep the whole lot onto the floor. (Incidentally, he occupied the only chair; the children either stood, or sat on the floor).

Regarding this 'clean sweep' tendency; I shall have occasion later on to mention that I exhibited it myself when all hope of winning a game of draughts had gone. An inherited characteristic no doubt.

However, to go back. Here was my father, orphaned at the age of seven. He was the youngest child of the family, and something had to be done.

By this time, most of his older brothers and sisters had left Ince. The decay of English rural life was already well advanced, and the rising generation were driven by low wages and unemployment to seek work in the neighbouring towns. They were even driven from Ince by lack of somewhere to live. All the land there was part of an estate, and not one square yard was ever made available for building.

There was however one older brother, Tom, still living there. Though very poor and already married, he took young William into his home and did his best for him. He even found the few coppers a week needed to send him to a private school - the cottage of the village tailor. This tailor did a little teaching at the same time as he plied his trade, and at any rate taught his pupils to read and write and do some very simple arithmetic, but nothing beyond addition and subtraction.

At the age of nine, father's education was held to be complete, and he worked on one of the local farms. He was wakened in the early hours of the morning, and I have heard him tell how, on one occasion when he hadn't come down to breakfast, he was found sitting on the bed, having fallen asleep in the act of putting his socks on. When he was old enough, probably at the age of about fourteen, he was apprenticed to a wheelwright.

I know very little of what happened in my father's boyhood and youth, chiefly because 'bedtime stories' were mother's job. However, I recall a few incidents which he mentioned at odd times, and which throw a little light on social conditions in a small Cheshire village about a hundred years ago.

There was no doctor in the village, but there was a dentist of sorts in the person of the village shoemaker, perhaps because he was one of the few people who possessed a pair of pliers. There was of course no nonsense about injections or gas. The cobbler did his best, but it seems likely that patients only sought his aid when the agony of an aching molar could be endured no longer. Not infrequently the tooth broke off in the course of extraction, and the painful business had to be started all over again.

Not all villages possessed an idiot, though they must have been common enough a century ago, the sad result of generations of inbreeding in isolated communities. There were no institutions as now where they could be cared for, or trained for some simple manual work if they were capable of it. They were in the nominal charge of relatives, but in practice they just roamed at large in the community.

Such a one was Sammy, who was living in Ince in the eighteen fifties. Two men in the pub once had a bet as to whether Sammy had sufficient sense to know that a threepenny bit was more valuable than a penny. The matter was soon put to the test. "Now Sammy," said the umpire as he laid two coins on the table, "Here's a threepenny bit and here's a penny. You can keep the one you choose. Which will you have?" Sammy didn't hesitate. "I'm noan goin' ter be greedy so I'll tak t'littlest," he said, and the loser had to pay the forfeit.

A 'hanging' at Chester was often made the occasion of a village holiday, for public executions were not abolished until 1868. Men and boys - I don't know about the women - trooped off to Chester taking with them what money they had saved, for outside the gaol was a fair where it could be spent in all sorts of ways. The highlight of course was the hanging. My father on one occasion saw four men hanged at once, and I remember a few of the lurid details. It doesn't strike one as having been a refined age.

Strangely, along with this coarseness and morbid pleasure in witnessing the suffering of others, there was an odd streak of religious intensity. A literal heaven and hell were much more present to the imagination in that day than in this, and youths - my father amongst them - who one day had been attending an execution in Chester might on the following day be holding a prayer meeting in the corner of a field. How far this was the result of genuine religious fervour and how far a fending off of possible future unpleasantness, is hard to say.

It was a superstitious age. A youth returning from choir practice late one evening was walking along a path which was parallel to a low hedge, skirting the churchyard. Walking about fifty yards behind him was the vicar. To the latter's great astonishment the youth suddenly threw up one arm, clenched his fist and shouted "Sattan [Satan] a' defy thee. A' defy thee Sattan. Ah'm a Psaum singer i' Thornton church and a' defy thee!" However, at this point he was evidently unable to maintain his defiance any longer, for he took to his heels and ran. The vicar was at first at a loss to account for the chorister's sudden vision of the Evil One, until he looked over the hedge. There, dimly in the mist, he could see a pair of horns slowly rising and falling, though the contentedly grazing cow to which they belonged was effectively concealed by the hedge.

***The Railway Bridge under construction, 1886***
*Father was employed on the construciton of the wooden supports and shuttering.*

*H.F. Starkey*

It was not at all uncommon for a young man who had just finished his apprenticeship to be told that there was no longer any work for him. As an apprentice he cost his employer practically nothing, but once he was 'out of his time' he could claim full journeyman's wages. This happened to my father as soon as he could no longer be employed economically for half a crown a quarter, and he found himself looking for a job. Nothing offered locally, but a big new railway bridge was being built across the Mersey joining Runcorn to Widnes, and he heard there was a demand for skilled labour there. He was strictly speaking a wheelwright, but thought he might have a chance of being taken on as a carpenter, and his hopes were realised.

In Runcorn he had a sister Mary, one of the older members of the family who had forsaken the country for the town years before because Ince had so little to offer. She was married to one Walter Collier and they kept a grocer's shop. It is still in being though it has changed hands and has now come into the possession of its ancient rival, the 'Co-op'. It is in Church Street, near Public Hall Street.

Incidentally this couple had a son, Samuel Francis, who later became a famous name in Methodist circles as head of the Manchester Mission, 'Collier of Manchester', and who in 1913 was President of the Methodist Conference. But that is by the way and I must return to father, who has just arrived in Runcorn with his tool bag and his modest bundle of personal possessions.

It was of course convenient for him to lodge with his sister Mary, and next door was Mr Sandford's shop, where a certain Sarah Watson had been credited with a long string of fourpences for the killing of rats!

They met under rather odd circumstances. As a result of some oversight, the back gate through which my father usually entered had been bolted, and he decided to climb over it. Unfortunately he slipped in doing so and though he fell on the inside he twisted his ankle and struggled to his feet in quite a lot of pain. From the other side of the fence, Sarah had seen the accident and was full of sympathy; the stage was set for romance.

They were soon very much in love and planning to get married. In those days engagements were not usually long, but their marriage was delayed because father hurt his shoulder severely in an accident on the bridge, and was unable to continue his employment. Their prospects were not very bright, but quite soon he was lucky enough to get a job as early morning postman at twelve shillings a week, and boldly venturing, took a little shop in which he sold milk, and butter of his own churning.

All seemed set fair, but there was still an obstacle. My father, though never taking drink to excess, was not a total abstainer. Mother on the other hand had an absolute horror of drink, probably because she had seen the effects of it in her own home as a child. They discussed the matter very seriously, but mother was firm, and finally told him that he must give up drink altogether or she would break off the engagement. Very wisely, father decided that although he could live without alcohol, he couldn't live without Sarah. He signed the pledge and except under medical advice during his last long illness, he never again took a drop of alcohol to the end of his life.

He knocked up a few odds and ends of furniture, and with twelve shillings a week certain, their youth and health, and what they could make out of the little milk business, my parents were married at Runcorn Parish Church on the 9th of September 1865. He was twenty four, and she was exactly two and half years younger.

# CHAPTER 3

# *From Hard Times to Easier*

Families were large in mid-Victorian times, but even by those standards the family into which I was born might fairly be described as out-size, for there were sixteen of us, including two pairs of twins. I was one of the younger members - actually the fourteenth - so it is only at second hand that I can give some account of the earlier married life of my parents.

When my father married, his only sure income was the twelve shillings a week he earned as a part-time postman. But the house to which my parents moved on their marriage was also a little shop, and here they sold milk, butter, and a few odds and ends of sweets and groceries. This probably brought their total income up to a pound a week or a little more.

No opportunity was lost of 'turning an honest penny', and father probably put his carpentering skills to good use because one of the older children later recalled that he made coffins, and they slept with the coffin boards propped up against the bedroom wall.

After they had been married for two or three years, a quite new line of employment opened up. An agent of the Prudential Assurance Company had been found guilty of embezzlement and sentenced to a term of imprisonment. His books were in hopeless disorder and the Company sent down a representative to straighten things out. He had no very easy task. The addresses of insured people were often wrong owing to removals not having been notified, and in many cases the money forwarded did not tally with the records. Father, as local postman, was able to give the representative a good deal of help, especially in the matter of addresses. At the end of it all the Prudential man asked him whether he would care to take over the agency; if so, he would be only too pleased to support an application.

Father must have hesitated. His education had been of the sketchiest, and he knew how important it was that the books should balance; an operation that would test to the limit his scanty knowledge of arithmetic.

However, he took it on, and found he was able to do the clerical work without serious difficulty. He was paid a percentage commission on the amount collected each week, and in addition there was a special commission for new business; 'fourteen times' as the rate then was. This meant that if he persuaded somebody to take out a policy for which the premium was threepence a week, he would receive a commission of fourteen times three pence, or three and sixpence. On the other hand if the policy 'lapsed' through the insured person falling behind with his premiums, father was debited with fourteen times the premium.

His 'book' - that is the weekly amount he was responsible for collecting - was at first very small, perhaps three pounds. His commission on the weekly collection was fifteen per cent or three shillings in the pound, which on a three pound book would bring him in nine shillings a week. He was very diligent in canvassing for new business, and in the course of years built up a book of twenty pounds, in those days the largest in Runcorn.

Incidentally, these small policies were know as 'Industrial Policies'. Their purpose was to cover the cost of burial, and were taken out on the birth of each child if at all possible. There was no Welfare State or anything like it. Working class families had their pride, and there was no more appalling disgrace than to end up in a pauper's grave.

After a round of collecting, his first job on reaching home was to balance his book against the cash in his pocket, and occasionally there was a small discrepancy which he found difficult to trace.

On one occasion he had spent several hours at this task, and when mother enquired what the trouble was, he explained that he was threepence short. She persuaded him to come and have his supper. "You'll feel fresh again afterwards," she said "and I expect you'll trace that threepence in no time at all."

While he was having his supper she had no difficulty in slipping a threepenny bit into his collection, admittedly a somewhat irregular method of securing a balance! Then, when the meal was over he returned to the task of straightening out the discrepancy. Naturally mother expected a quick and triumphant result, but an hour went by and he was still engaged in the struggle. "Does it still not come right?"

she asked anxiously. "Blowed if I can make it out at all," he answered. "It comes out threepence too much now!"

He never did trace that threepence, for mother never dared tell him of her well-meant guile, though she told her children after his death, and she took great care never to tamper with the collection again.

There is no doubt that father tended to worry over the details of his business, and mother didn't like to see him worried. Another of her somewhat unusual methods comes to mind, this time connected with bad payers.

Often in my teens, during the holidays, I would collect a round for my father, and I was struck with the high proportion of people who paid their premiums with strict regularity every week, well over ninety percent of them at a guess. In the frugal working-class household of Victorian days these regular amounts would be put back from the weekly wage packet, usually by the wife, and stored perhaps in a tin or old teapot until called for by the rent collector or insurance man.

But there were a few who for various reasons were apt to slip behind, and father nursed these cases very carefully. He had a list of the worst of them, and would make a special call on a Saturday afternoon, whilst the week's wages were likely to be comparatively intact. Mother would keep in sympathetic touch with the situation, and would make a special note of cases in which, first, the defaulter lived not far away, secondly, the premium was small, and lastly, father had little hope of getting it. Her method may be illustrated by the typical case of Mrs Slackly, premium fivepence a week.

Mother would slip out unobtrusively to the lady in question and soon get down to business. Having ascertained that there was not a hope of the premium being forthcoming she would say, "You see Mrs Slackly, you have no idea how my husband worries over cases like yours. Now listen! To save him worry, I'm going to give you that fivepence if you will promise to pay him when he comes. It's a secret between us, of course. You won't let me down will you?"

Mrs Slackly gave the necessary promise. Later, when father returned from what was always a rather depressing round, his report was something like "Well Sarah, I never do very well with these Saturday afternooners as you know, but I had one real surprise. Mrs Slackly paid up her fivepence almost before I had time to ask for it!" and mother felt that the pleasure it gave him was cheaply earned at the cost of fivepence.

Mrs Slackly could of course have kept the fivepence and mother could have done nothing about it, but she was seldom if ever let down in this way. The practice cannot be recommended for it could rarely have resulted in any long term improvement but it was typical of her desire, whenever she could, to add a little to the happiness of those around her.

Father spared no effort and the business was slowly increasing, but the family was increasing too, and I have heard mother say that at one time she had 'two that couldn't walk and two that couldn't talk'. For a period of some years times must have been very hard indeed; hard to the point of tragedy. I find I can give very few details. For one thing I was almost the last of the family, and when I was born the hardest part of the struggle was over. Further, it had resulted in such consequences that mother could seldom bear to refer to those earlier days.

The terrible fact was that, between 1867 and 1879, eight of her children died. It was a fearful toll, bearing in mind that both parents were of sturdy physique, as were the surviving children. The eight who were lost were healthy and normal when born, and I know how hard mother would have struggled for the life of her babies. Why then did so many die?

With one exception (a sad drowning accident) they all died of infectious diseases, five of scarlet fever and two of measles. These diseases were far more deadly eighty years ago than they are today, but nevertheless, if home conditions had been easier there would certainly have been more survivors. Both parents were much overworked, and could scarcely have had the energy to cope with a situation that was difficult at best.

Moreover, medical knowledge was in its infancy as to how infectious diseases were caused, how they were spread, and how they should be treated. There were no isolation hospitals, nor any possibility of nursing cases under conditions of isolation in a small and overcrowded house. It is significant that after 1879, by which time the grim struggle with poverty had somewhat eased, there were no further deaths.

I have heard mother say that although epidemics of scarlet fever were frequent and severe, their own home suffered more than most.

She put this down to the fact that father's insurance work caused him every day to visit houses in which there were scarlet fever cases, and from there he brought the infection to his own family. I have since made enquiries on this point from a doctor friend, and he tells me it would be quite possible for a man to be himself immune from the disease, and yet to carry the germs in his nose and throat and be a source of infection to others.

Though mother never talked very much about the days of struggle, odd incidents came out now and then. One little episode related to their very early married life, when mother's first confinement was imminent and they were about to become the proud parents of twin daughters. They were running their little milk shop and on this particular occasion they had been up at four in the morning as usual to do the churning, and mother had worked non-stop all day and far into the evening. At last all the jobs were finished, and she could sit down and relax. "Eh, Will, but I am tired," she said, as she put her feet up. Now father was in no way a hard man, but he evidently felt there could be too much pandering to feminine frailty. "Lass," he said, "Tha's always tired!"

The average interval between successive births was only about eighteen months, and on one occasion mother was in the shop actually serving when the latest arrival was but four days old.

In those early days there was one line in which mother took a special interest: the making up of 'lucky bags' which sold at a halfpenny each. For those not acquainted with the term, let me explain that a lucky bag consisted of a paper bag containing a little assortment of sweets, biscuits and nuts. Now and again the 'lucky' purchaser would find a small toy or brooch or other little oddment.

Lucky bag sales were certainly brisk, and mother had a job to keep pace with the demand. Anxious to learn the secret of such remarkable success, father decided to investigate. He found that she had been making up the bags with a much too generous hand, with the result that he was making a loss on every one! She agreed that this couldn't go on and was persuaded to keep the quota per bag to reasonable limits. No doubt sales tailed off a bit after that, but I daresay her over-plump lucky bags had served as a good advertising line.

Though my parents never became comfortably off, poverty did begin to relax its grip as the years went by. Father's 'book' steadily increased, the work of collecting and canvassing became a full-time job, and he was able to give up first his little dairy business and then his postal work.

I found out years afterwards that he was much more than a collector. He was 'guide, philosopher and friend' to scores of people he visited. At any time he might be asked how to make a will, or what would be a good name for the new baby, or what sort of job he would advise for their Tom who would soon be leaving school. Once, he told me, a woman asked him whether she should accept a proposal of marriage she had received. She was a widow of about forty with a little property of her own.

"Mrs Wilkes," said father, "I don't really think you want my advice. You have already made up your mind to accept him now haven't you? But I tell you plainly, if you marry Harry Brindley you'll be sorry. All he's after is what you've got. He drinks more than is good for him and he's lazy, so that when work's short he's one of the first to be sacked. " This was plain warning enough but just the same she married him and the sequel was not without a touch of comedy.

Brindley turned out to be all that father had said and worse, and after about a year his wife wished to leave him. However, she also wished to secure her furniture and personal possessions, so she secretly arranged to rent an empty house which was quite close by. The next act in the drama had to await the following Saturday afternoon, when Brindley came home, very drunk as usual, lay down on the sofa and soon fell fast asleep. This was what she was waiting for, and by pre-arrangement three neighbours and their husbands began moving the furniture into her new house. Unfortunately the operation was only about half completed when Brindley woke up, slowly took in what was going on and tried to put a stop to the proceedings. The three husbands thereupon sat on him on the sofa until the women had finished the job, (except, presumably for the removal of the sofa!).

Meanwhile, strongly resenting his uncomfortable position and the steady disappearance of the furniture, Brindley cursed and swore, using the vilest language, until one of the women brought a policeman to the scene. He took down in his notebook generous samples of the language, with the result that Brindley was summoned in due course and given a maximum fine for using obscene language within the hearing of the public.

It must have been in the late seventies that father hit upon a profitable sideline. He would order from a colliery one, and sometimes two, ten-ton wagon-loads of coal, which were directed to him at the railway goods yard. On his insurance rounds he would book orders for coal, usually half a ton or a ton, and these orders he would send to a carter by the name of Moores in Sutherland Street. In this way he bought and sold coal with the minimum of effort, usually without even seeing it. He sold only the best coal, and I well remember that the price was sixteen and threepence a ton. I never knew how much he made in this way, but I have heard him say that when the 'Co-op' entered the coal business he found himself worse off by fifteen shillings a week. He might well have lost half his customers, in which case he must previously have been making thirty shillings a week.

His total income now, about 1879, with the commission on his enlarged 'book' and on new business together with what he obtained by buying and selling coal, was probably in the region of five pounds a week. This is only guesswork, because in Victorian times personal income ranked almost with the facts of life as a matter for the strictest reticence. But assuming it was five pounds a week, which doesn't sound very much now, it compares very favourably with the thirty shillings a week earned by the skilled artisan.

He and my mother had now been married for fourteen years. They had been faced with a grim struggle, and it had not been without heartbreaking loss, but they had survived it. Even with the expense of so many children they could be reasonably comfortable, so father bought a house in Leinster Gardens where there was better accommodation for his still-increasing family. Now at last they had reached the 'easier times' which they both so truly deserved.

*The National School in Church Street*

CHAPTER 4

# The Infants School

I have a very clear recollection of my fourth birthday, because it brought with it a shilling box of bricks and a sixpenny gun which would fire a wooden bullet at least two yards. Such outstanding events naturally leave a strong impression.

Of earlier events I remember only a few, one being an unsuccessful attempt at bird catching. I had asked how this could be done, and mother told me that all I had to do was to put a little salt on their tails, and she supplied me with a quantity of salt. The birds were definitely unco-operative, and after many fruitless efforts extending over half the morning, I gave it up. I explained to mother that you couldn't put salt on a bird's tail unless you had first caught the bird, and she agreed that there might be something in that way of looking at it. Meanwhile she had enjoyed an hour or two's freedom from a rather pestering small boy.

I remember too when Mrs Rolls upset the cup of tea. Mrs Rolls was an old lady who often came along to do a bit of patching and darning on a Thursday afternoon, and she used to stay to tea. One day she had the little accident just mentioned, and knowing from personal experience how unpopular I suddenly became on such occasions, I thought, "Now she'll catch it! Clean cloth too!" I could hardly believe my ears when what I heard was something like "Now don't bother about it Mrs Rolls. After tea I'll just pop it in to soak and it'll all come out!" I'm afraid I was really disappointed and after our visitor had gone I asked mother why she didn't tell Mrs Rolls that she was a very naughty lady. Mother explained how important it was to make visitors feel happy and at their ease, though she probably didn't use just those words.

Soon after my fourth birthday I began to attend the Infant Department of the National School. It was a Church of England school, but we all went there because it was the nearest one to home. I was escorted by my brother William, who attended the Boys' School adjoining the Infants'. I can still recall some of the incidents connected with that first day, no doubt because it was the first day. After the morning hymn and a prayer, we had a scripture lesson. It consisted of a very exciting story I had not heard before, about two cities which were very wicked, so God sent down fire and brimstone from heaven which burnt them up, but there were a few good people who escaped. These good people were told that on no account must they look back, but one of them, the wife of a man called Lot, thought she would like just a peep, so she turned round and was at once turned into a pillar of salt. I thought that this was rather hard, just for one little peep.

At this point a bell rang, and I soon found that this marked the end of a lesson. The teacher began to talk about something else, numbers such as 1 and 2 and 4, but my mind was far away. I remember her saying: "Why aren't you listening, Walter Littler?" (for some reason in the Infants' School we were always addressed by our full name). I brought my attention back with difficulty to my present surroundings. "I was thinking about that poor woman who was turned into salt," I explained.

I tried to listen to what she was telling us about numbers but I soon lost interest and got up and began to walk away. "Here, where are you going?" the teacher asked. I said politely that I had now had enough and was going home. To my surprise I found that this was not allowed. It was my first taste of any discipline other than parental.

Playtime came, which I quite enjoyed, then more lessons, and at last a bell rang very loudly and we were really allowed to go home. I was rather annoyed to find brother William waiting for me outside. I told him that I was quite able to find my own way home, and that this was not to happen again. But it did happen again - that very afternoon! This was more than flesh and blood could stand. It had been raining, and I told him that if he didn't go away I would sit down in that puddle of water, indicating one that had collected in the rather uneven flagstones. William smirked. That decided it, and I carried out my threat. He dragged me along and I resisted, but he was a well-grown seven and a half and managed to keep me firmly in tow. I reached home with the seat of my trousers soaked. William stated the case for the prosecution, with the result that I was found guilty and sent to bed until my trousers could be dried. The process seemed to take a long time.

Very soon afterwards I must have been allowed to make my own way home because I don't remember any further trouble.

I had not been attending school long before I began to hear from other boys in the playground, words I had never heard before. They were possessed of a wonderful vigour, most of them beginning with what I later discovered to be the letter B. I was thrilled, and had soon mastered a good selection of such desirable acquisitions to the vocabulary. Yes, I must certainly display them at the first opportunity. Just wait till I got home!

On arriving home I found my sister Nellie, who was twelve, alone in the kitchen. "Hello Walter," she said, "had a good afternoon? I expect you're ready for your tea. "

"Yes, you b***** b*****," I replied.

"What's that you said?" she almost screamed.

"I only said yes, you b***** b*****," I replied, rather taken aback at this violent reaction.

"Mother, Mother!" Nellie was running down the passage, and by this time I was really scared, unable to understand what all the fuss was about. Mother came, but she wasn't angry. She just explained that most words were good, but there were some bad ones. To use them was called swearing, and nice little boys didn't swear. It seemed a pity, but if mother said they were bad words that was the end of the matter, and I allowed my new possession to rust for lack of use. Though I don't actually remember her employing it, this would be one of the occasions when she would make use of a favourite quotation: "Evil communications corrupt good manners. "

Returning once more to the subject of life at school, I have already referred to the teaching of scripture. If my own reaction was typical, and I think it was, the Bible stories were very popular. But we didn't always have stories. Sometimes we learnt by heart, repeating after the teacher one Bible verse for each letter of the alphabet. F for instance stood for 'Freely ye have received, freely give'. *G* was for 'God is love'. *H*, I have forgotten, but *I* was for 'I am the way, the truth and the life'.

In most respects modern methods of education show a great advance on those in use some seventy years ago, but not I am sure in this matter of repetition. It is supposed to be boring, and for the teacher no doubt it is, but small children love it. They are doing something, and the diffident ones gain increased confidence as they feel their own uncertainties corrected by the chorus of voices around them.

For scripture we had nothing except some rather moth-eaten pictures. There was Abraham about to offer up Isaac, Saul with his javelin poised to hurl at the minstrel David, and others which I do not now recall.

For writing we had slates, never paper. On one side these were ruled with lines, and on the other there were squares. These were scratched on, and permanent. I wish I could say that the slate was cleaned by means of a small damp sponge attached to the corner of the slate by a short string, but it just would not be true. The method used was effective, but hardly in keeping with modern standards of hygiene.

Our writing lessons began by drawing a series of pot-hooks, and one could actually *hear* when the class was writing, especially if, as often happened, somebody had a squeaky pencil. From pot-hooks we were soon promoted to letters, and this greatly increased our sense of importance. Later came the great day when the teacher wrote on the blackboard, very clearly, a column of printed words: bat, cat, fat. She pointed to the letters and following her lead we announced in happy chorus that:

    b-a-t spells bat

    c-a-t spells cat

    f-a-t spells fat, and so on.

We were reading! (well almost reading, anyway). No doubt better methods are in use today, but this one served us well enough. For most of us though, it was a far cry from the stage just described to that at which we could read, very haltingly, a simple passage of one syllable words in some small, limp-backed books we used. Few children had reached the stage of fluent reading even when they passed out of the Infants' School at the age of six. In this respect I was lucky, because I seemed to reach the fluent stage very quickly. I received a good deal of help at home and with books available I was always pushing ahead, eager to 'find out what happened'!

While on this subject, I have very little first-hand knowledge of the methods used in teaching children today, but it is a fact that illiteracy was so common during the conscription period after the Second World War that the army had to organise special classes to deal with it; and all of the men concerned were of sufficient mental capacity to pass the minimum requirements for military training. In my boyhood it could be said that illiteracy was unheard of amongst normal children who were in regular attendance at school.

I have spoken vaguely of 'the teacher'. It didn't take me many days to get familiar with the staff, and I still remember them very distinctly. At a desk in the middle of a long schoolroom was the headmistress, Miss Highfield, much in evidence at the opening and closing of school. There were two lady assistants, Miss Carr and Miss Goodwell, and two pupil teachers aged perhaps fifteen or sixteen; Bertha Millington and Hetty Waterworth. At least, that is what we called them in conversation with one another. In addressing them we would simply say "Please teacher. "

In those days of course I knew nothing about the various grades and qualifications of teachers, but I became better informed as I grew older.

The pupil teachers were apprenticed at a minimum age of fourteen. They often began with a probationary year when they were only thirteen, but they could not be formally apprenticed until they were fourteen. They had a tiny salary of perhaps eight pounds a year, rising a little for each of the four years of their service. During this time they learnt the technique of teaching by helping one of the senior mistresses and at the same time they pursued a course of study in English, Geography, History, Mathematics, and perhaps one or two other subjects. The necessary tuition was given by the headmistress, usually between eight and nine in the morning, and in the evening they would spend two or three hours doing work she had set them which had to be produced on the following day. It must have been a terrible life for a young girl.

After a year they had to sit for a first year examination at Chester, and similarly for second and third year examinations. At the end of the fourth year they took the 'Queen's Scholarship', in which there were many levels of success. If they passed at a sufficiently high level they were entitled to take an assisted course at a Training College, and after a further two years there, take a final examination and pass out as 'Trained Certificated'. Probably Miss Highfield was of this grade. Those who passed but at a lower level were graded 'Article 50's'. They then had a choice. They could continue their teaching career at that level, or they could by tuition and/or correspondence course take an examination of equal difficulty to that set at the Training Colleges. If they passed they were then graded 'Certificated', which for obvious reasons had not quite the same cachet as 'Trained Certificated'. Probably Miss Goodwell and Miss Carr were of this grade, though it is only guesswork.

Besides these three grades of teachers there was still another, defined in Article 68 of the Education Code. The definition is cloaked in much verbiage, but the popular description seems to have been not far wide of the mark: 'A man or woman who has been vaccinated and has attained the age of eighteen years'. They were commonly known as 'Article 68's'. We had none in the Infants' School I attended, but I was to meet with the male of the species at a later stage of my education.

Salaries were appallingly low, even by the standards of those days. The average for a certificated woman teacher in a Church of England School such as ours was forty six pounds a year, while the average for a head teacher was seventy two pounds. In many cases however, especially in country schools, she would live rent free in the school house. Salaries in Board of Education Schools were considerably higher.

The old system vanished long ago, and the pupil teachers with it. To a present day student, enjoying as she does a full and varied life apart from her work, it must seem incredible that these girls were willing to endure such slavery for a mere pittance. To those of us who were living at that time it doesn't seem so strange. People hoped for so little. Long hours of work were normal, and the pupil teacher was not made envious by comparisons as she bent her thin shoulders to the grim task of earning a meagre living in a respected profession, if marriage should not be offered her.

Staff accommodation was primitive in the extreme. There was no staff room. If Miss Highfield had to interview a parent, it could only be at her desk in full view of the whole school. As the teachers entered school they hung their hats and cloaks on a rack just by the door. There was not much privacy even about the staff toilet, which was just the end one of a row, the others being used by the children.

There were four classes, one at the East end of the schoolroom and another in the middle, while a third occupied a gallery which stretched across the West end. The fourth class, the 'babies', had a room to itself. I was always to associate the gallery with sewing lessons and also, oddly enough with coconuts; but all that was to come later.

We had a sewing lesson almost on my first day. I have never heard before or since of a school where sewing was included in the curriculum for small boys, but in the Education Code for 1890 - obtained with some difficulty - there sure enough it is, set out as an alternative to drawing, the two being classed conveniently together as 'handwork'.

But to return to my first sewing lesson. If it taught me nothing else it taught me the meaning of fear. Each of us was supplied with a piece of calico, perhaps seven inches by three, with one long side turned down to the depth of about half an inch to form a hem. This was kept in place by a few very large tacking stitches and our job was to sew it neatly. I cannot now remember whether we had a thimble.

The first time I attempted the task, my stitches were much too small, and when most of the others had finished about half the length, I had completed only an inch or so. At this point the teacher came round to see how we were getting on. At most of the specimens she gave just a glance and passed on, but she paused at mine. It evidently demanded closer scrutiny. "You naughty, lazy little boy," she said. "You have hardly done anything at all!" and she slapped me, with considerable vigour. In carrying out this process the teacher would hold the child's hand, palm downwards with her own left hand, while she slapped the back of its wrist with the other. It was much more than just a token tap; it was quite painful.

I nursed my hand. The teacher passed on and I pondered the situation. Light suddenly dawned. Of course! I had been making stitches that were much too small! That could soon be put right. I got to work with great enthusiasm and had soon finished; finished before anybody else. I raised by hand to attract her attention and said "Please teacher, I've finished!" "That just shows what you can do when you're not lazy," she said, and came along to inspect. "Oh, what great big ugly stitches!" The beginnings of a smile quickly faded, and I received another slapping.

My thoughts were of the gloomiest. Small stitches or big stitches, I should be slapped no matter which I used. And there would be another sewing lesson tomorrow, and the day after that, and the day after that. .

I saw life as one long succession of sewing lessons accompanied by a corresponding succession of slappings. I just wept.

Meanwhile the lesson had ended, and the teacher was gathering up the calico work and the needles. I sat on, scarcely noticing, so preoccupied was I with these terrible forebodings. "What are you crying for, Walter Littler?" she asked as she came to collect from me. "I'm thinking about tomorrow's sewing lesson," I sobbed. She made no comment.

But tomorrow, there wasn't a sewing lesson. No doubt it was not included in the timetable for every day. When the next one did come round, having received some instruction from mother in the meantime, I managed quite reasonably well and attracted no further slappings. Many a time since, when I have been inclined to worry over some impending trouble, the moral of that sewing lesson that never happened has saved me the loss of a night's sleep.

Certainly this pupil teacher had been rather cruel, but one has to bear in mind the conditions under which she worked. It is small wonder that her nerves were frayed. She faced her day's teaching after a long evening's study and early morning lessons, and she and one certificated teacher were responsible between them for the supervision of ninety children. (The certificated teacher was held by the Code to be sufficient for sixty or seventy children, and the pupil teacher for a further thirty.)

In many cases, another factor worked against them. These girls often had poor but ambitious parents who wanted something better for them than 'service', or working in a shop or factory, but with many other mouths to feed the nutrition was frequently poor, and this was long before the days of diet supplements. They were often anaemic and in no state to sustain such a punishing regime.

The children, sitting uncomfortably and fidgeting on a gallery, were so young that the mopping up of puddles was almost routine, and plenty of tasks more unpleasant than that fell to the lot of the luckless assistant.

A little way back I also mentioned that the gallery had an association with coconuts. It arose in this way. From somewhere or other father had bought a sackful of coconuts which had been dumped in the back yard. They attracted my special notice because the outer husk surrounding the shell was still on them and later that day I became aware of a striking resemblance between Bertha Millington's head and the husky outside of these coconuts.

Accordingly I said to my neighbour Ernest Jones, "Isn't Bertha Millington's head like the outside of a coconut?" To my horror, he replied "I shall tell teacher. " Up went his hand, and he said "Please teacher, Walter Littler says Bertha Millington's head's like a coconut. Please teacher, Walter Littler says. . . " he simply repeated the allegation again and again.

The danger to me was not immediate, for eighty children shuffling and talking on that gallery produced such background noise that the teacher had not yet heard of the interesting comparison between her head and a coconut. I tried to bribe Ernest with promises of sweets tomorrow, but all in vain. What was worse, other children in the neighbourhood were taking up the refrain, and in a very short time seven or eight voices were chanting in unison "Please teacher Walter Littler says Bertha Millington's head is like a coconut. Please teacher Walter Littler says. . . "

At last the young lady in question heard the chorus and bore down upon the group that was chanting it. I was soon asked for an explanation, and I told her that my father had just bought some *very nice looking* coconuts and it was just that they had a lot of hair. . . please, I hadn't meant to be rude. . .

I think I must have got away with it for I don't remember any slapping. But what dreadful tell-tales!

Small children are like that. I never taught any as young as five, but I have occasionally taught children of eight, and they are almost as bad. You ask the class "Who has been throwing ink pellets?" and from half a dozen directions comes the answer "Please sir, it was Tommy Wilson. " Children of ten think this is rather hitting below the belt, but when you put your question they will stare fixedly at Tommy Wilson, and Tommy is your man! At aged twelve or so you have to press quite hard to get any information, and with boys older still, Tommy is quite safe as far as they are concerned. 'Splitting' would represent a quite unpardonable breach of their code of honour.

I have described the slapping process, and this was the normal form of punishment. Miss Highfield was the only one who ever used the cane.

A punishment which I witnessed only occasionally was the 'Dunce's Cap'. This was just like the dunce's cap of the picture books, a very tall, cone-shaped hat made of brown paper with DUNCE chalked clearly across it. Presumably it was just mental slowness that was being treated as a crime. The practice ought never to have been allowed, and was probably dying out even in my time.

In summer when there were no fires, a quite common punishment was to make the offender stand for a while inside the fireguard. I remember quite a lively sequel to this, the dramatis personae being the delinquent John Owen, the headmistress, Miss Highfield, and one of the pupil teachers, Bertha Millington of coconut memory. I should say that although it was easy to knock the fireguard over and escape for a few seconds, such a practice was no longer favoured, because recapture was swift with a slapping by way of additional bonus.

On this occasion however, close by the class at the East end of the room a lot of forms had been placed side by side, probably to make a platform for some sort of public function on the previous evening. With nothing else to do but look around, John had seized upon the strategic possibilities of the arrangement. One had only to crawl under those forms to find oneself in a most inviting cave, far more interesting than the rotten old fireguard!

He acted quickly. Over went the fireguard, and he started on his run to the haven of refuge perhaps fifteen yards away.

The noise of the falling fireguard had attracted everyone's notice including that of Miss Highfield, who was sitting at her desk quite close. She was in hot pursuit in a moment, and a short but most spirited race ensued. We watched this breathlessly, all our sympathies naturally with John. He had an initial lead of two or three yards, but Miss Highfield had the longer legs and was certainly gaining. To our great relief John was the winner. He dived into the space below the forms, Miss Highfield only just failing to grasp the second of his disappearing ankles. Anxious to increase his margin of safety, John crawled along to the wall at the far end. In the dim light we could just make out his small figure. How jolly to be under there! How we envied him!

It was a great disappointment to us that Miss Highfield didn't continue the pursuit, but no doubt she felt that her dignity was involved, and after a short pause she returned to her desk. Morning school would end in half an hour or so. What would happen then?

At twelve o'clock, Miss Highfield must have thought it was time the situation was terminated. This involved negotiation, and it was here that Bertha Millington came in as Ambassador Extraordinary. Standing at the spot where John's second leg had had such a narrow escape, Miss Highfield whispered something to Bertha. The latter knelt down, bent her head so as to be able to speak into the cave, and said "John Owen, Miss Highfield says *you have been a very naughty boy.* However, you may come out now and go home, and she has promised not to punish you." John was soon out, victor over the Establishment for the first time ever. He must have felt it had been a wonderful morning!

I have already referred to some of the subjects we took: scripture, reading, writing and sewing, but there were others, with arithmetic well to the fore. It was done on the 'squared' side of the slate, because this helped us to keep the figures in orderly rows and columns. Before we left the Infants' at the age of six, we could do some simple addition, and we could subtract, provided that each number on the top line was bigger than the one below it. A lot of attention was paid to multiplication tables which we chanted in chorus, up to 'five times'.

Then there was 'drill', when we stood about a yard apart in the big schoolroom and did little bending and stretching exercises. All this was done rhythmically, sometimes to the click-click of a 'signal', sometimes to a simple tune on the piano. (There never seemed to be any lack of teachers who could play it).

Marching was always a great feature of Infant School life. We marched everywhere, whether we were coming in from the playground after the morning break or dismissing at the end of morning and afternoon school, and we always marched to the click-click of the 'signal', or to the piano.

We had no drawing lessons which seems strange, for children take readily to primitive forms of drawing, and certainly we did no work with crayons. But I have most vivid and painful memories of learning to knit, a subject for which I seemed to have even less natural aptitude than sewing.

I imagine the experiment of teaching knitting to a whole class at once must have been tried and found unsatisfactory, for certainly we were taught in pairs. The teacher, Miss Boxem, would arrange for two of us to stand on a form in front of the class, each equipped with a pair of needles and what was called 'cotton', though it looked like thin wool. In the course of the lesson she would teach these two to knit. The next day they would work in the class as knitters, while two more would be taught. Those who had not yet learnt to knit could do anything they liked with slate and pencil as long as they were quiet, and in silent reproach to the Education Code, most of them drew. Steadily the proportion of knitters grew, until the whole class had acquired the art.

I had looked forward to learning to knit, and rejoiced when my turn came. My joy was short lived!

My co-learner was Sam Royle, and he seemed to get on famously. With me, things went wrong almost from the start. I was presented with a piece of knitting of which only a few lines had been done, the top line consisting of ten stitches. Miss Boxem knitted one line slowly, and I watched with interest what seemed almost a juggler's trick; stitch after stitch disappearing from one needle and appearing on the other. "Now," she said "watch me while I do just one stitch, slowly, and then you can do one." To me it seemed a highly complex proceeding, but the attempt had to be made.

"You silly boy, you are putting your needle through the wrong stitch!" I put this little matter right, but such self-confidence as I possessed was rapidly ebbing away. "Now put the cotton round the needle, as you saw me do." I put it round, but unfortunately I had selected the wrong needle. "Are you just *trying* to be awkward?" she asked, accompanying her query with a smart slap on the side of the head.

From then on it was hopeless. Miss Boxem became more and more out of temper, and expressed her feelings by giving me a slap, sometimes on one side of the head, sometimes on the other. I thought that terrible lesson would never end, but at last (blessed sound!) the bell rang. Her final remark was that she had never before had a boy who hadn't learnt to knit in one lesson. Certainly Sam Royle seemed to be doing wonderfully and he hadn't received a single slap.

I reached home in a dreadful state and poured out my tale of woe to mother. She made me have my tea, and when I had finished it she took out a pair of needles and some wool, and began to teach me.

What a difference! If I made a mistake all I heard was "There, you nearly got it that time! Just let me show you where you went a little bit wrong. " In ten minutes or so I could knit, and wanted to do little else for the rest of the evening.

The following afternoon I soon satisfied Miss Boxem that I had had some instruction from my mother and could now knit, and she was glad enough to let me take my place beside Sam Royle and the other graduates.

Years later, when I was myself a teacher, I benefited from the experience. In my case it was no mere text-book maxim that fear produces a degree of mental paralysis, and therefore retards the process of learning. I learnt it the hard way. It was an unshakeable conviction acquired with tears in the remote past when I stood on a form trying to learn to knit.

After the painful start that I have described, the knitting lessons passed pleasantly enough. We never did anything but plain knitting, using two needles, and always with ten stitches. Eventually we had a sort of 'garter', but in the course of a lesson we could do only about two inches. Anyone who at the end of the lesson had achieved much less than that would be slapped for laziness. I received one such slapping, and I hadn't been lazy, either. It happened in this way.

The process of knitting consisted, as it seemed to me, in transferring stitches from one needle to the other. For some mysterious reason this transfer was accompanied by growth, but the essential thing was the transfer.

One day I had a brilliant idea. Why make the transfer in the cumbrous way we had been taught? Why not withdraw the needle gently from the ten stitches and thread them carefully onto the other? Just go on doing this, forward and backward, forward and backward, and one could get through this knitting business in half the time. I wondered that nobody had ever thought of such a simple plan before. I set to work accordingly, and was able to make the transfer at least twice as fast as my neighbours who were using the old-fashioned method.

After a few transfers I looked at my 'garter': ye-es, it was growing nicely, (a good example of wishful thinking!). A second inspection some time later left me just a little uneasy, and after a third, still later, not even wishful thinking could conceal the horrible truth - my knitting wasn't growing a bit, and now I should have nothing to show! I began to knit at frenzied speed in the old-fashioned style, but all too soon Miss

Boxem came round, my lack of progress stood revealed, and justice was administered.

Of course now and again we dropped a stitch, but we never worried about that. We just 'split a stitch' to make the number up to ten again, and that was that. Even at the time this method seemed to me rather unsatisfactory, and I have learnt since that it is definitely frowned upon in the best knitting circles.

Besides sewing and knitting, we sometimes did 'mat weaving', I don't remember much about it, but there was a square base of brown paper, so prepared that strips of coloured paper could be placed across it in one direction, and then other coloured strips could be passed over and under as though one were darning, in a direction at right angles to the first. The strips were manipulated by a special needle. It was rather pretty work, and the only thing we did that went any way towards satisfying a small child's creative instinct.

One of the most popular lessons was singing, and the songs chosen were mostly nursery rhymes set to music: 'Froggy would a-wooing go', 'Jack and Jill', 'Humpty Dumpty' and a few others. It was with singing too that our day closed, our evening hymn being the one still well-known to most children: 'Now the day is over'. We finished on a peaceful note, whatever the vicissitudes of the day that lay behind us.

By the kindness of the present headmistress, Miss Randles, I was able a few weeks ago to spend some time in the Infants' School of which I have been writing. What a difference! My first impression was one of brightness and colour, in contrast to the drabness I remembered. Various features contributed to this: light, attractive paintwork, coloured pictures hanging on the walls, vases of flowers here and there, and crayon drawings done by the children pinned to a screen. The classes were much smaller, and that gallery of certain painful memories had gone altogether. In its place are two brightly-furnished classrooms, with rocking horses, other large toys and creative playthings of every sort. Miss Randles tells me that the children really love their school, and I can well believe it.

It was a cheering visit, one to be recommended to anybody who has lost faith in the reality of human progress. I was glad to have made it.

CHAPTER 5

# Big Lads's

At the age of six, having spent two years in the Infant School, we were now due for transfer to the Boys' Department in the same block of buildings. With the feeling that we were now very important people we lined up in the Infant School, and under the direction of our teachers marched into that strange new world known to us as 'Big Lads's'. Other events of that day are still clear. First, our new teacher Mr Rhodes was standing at a desk calling us up one by one, and asking us our name, age and birthday. We managed this easily enough but some of us stuck over the question "What is your father's first name?" Quite unreasonably as it seemed to us, he wasn't satisfied with the answer "Mister," but in most cases he got what he wanted by asking "What does your mother call him?" If this failed, the boy was given a note to take home.

Hitherto all our work had been done on slates. These would continue to be used, but sometimes we would write on paper with pen and ink, news which gave a further boost to this pleasant new sensation of 'Grown-upness'. Mr Rhodes said we ought really to have a satchel, with proper straps to go over our shoulders. But these cost a shilling, and we couldn't have them unless our parents were willing to buy them. I remember being very anxious about this. A shilling satchel would be the very last word!

No wonder our heads were turned! I don't know about the other boys, but I recall how, when we were repeating a multiplication table after Mr Rhodes, I tried to make my voice sound as *deep* as possible, as became a member of Big Lads's.

At a quarter to two we turned up again for afternoon school, and Mr Rhodes called the new register. There was some discrepancy, and it had to be called all over again. This time it came right and he said if he, Mr Rhodes, hadn't found the mistake, he would have had to pay twenty pounds! This produced a horror-struck silence which could almost be felt. We were overwhelmed at the possibility of such a disaster, but as I recall the incident now, my mental comment is "Oh, Mr Rhodes, what a whopper!"

I was to be seven years in Big Lads's, but no other day stands out with anything like the clearness of that first one.

It did not take me long to get to know the staff. The Headmaster was Mr Jordan, usually called 'The Gaffer', or 'Gaffer Jordan'. Long before leaving school I had come to realise vaguely that he was a man of outstanding character and considerable culture. He belonged to that small band of men who are to be found in all ages and under all conditions of service; a born teacher devoted to his profession. He could have earned far more in some other occupation, but he had chosen the life he wanted in spite of the paucity of the remuneration; his salary was only a hundred and twenty pounds a year.

He had six or seven assistants, of whom only one or two would be 'Trained Certificated'. From this high point, qualifications trailed off through 'Untrained Certificated' and 'Article 50's' to finish up with a pupil teacher, in this case a youth of sixteen.

The average salary for a certificated assistant was only sixty seven pounds a year, at a time when even a skilled artisan earned eighty. Against this one has to set shorter working hours, longer holidays and - most important of all - security of employment. In those days, prior to 1906 and the first National Insurance Act, unemployment was the dread of every working class home, leaving as it did only the alternatives of 'selling up' and the workhouse, or slow starvation.

In this brief review of the staff, I find I have failed to mention the representative of one other category; Mr Jones was an 'Article 68'. He had the two essential qualifications referred to in the last chapter, but that was not his only asset. He showed great resource in concealing from his pupils the gaps in his own education.

He had sole charge of Standard Five, and I well remember one grammar lesson when we were taking it in turns round the class to analyse sentences. All was going well until one boy stuck over a particular phrase; he clearly had no ideas on the subject. He tried one or two others including myself who were equally at a loss and we stoically prepared ourselves for a beating. To our amazement, Mr Jones took a magnanimous line. He ran his eye casually over the page with the air of the practised grammarian and then said in his slow, heavy dialect: "Well, it's askin' a bit mooch fer you lads ter tackle a thing like that. It's what we call a prepositional phrase. It 'ud be a year or two yet before I could make yer understand it. We'll leave it fer now. " I was to discover later that the phrase was quite a simple one from the grammatical point of view and certainly had nothing to do with prepositions!

But I am getting on too fast and we must return to Standard One. After two years with Mr Rhodes - the man who came so near to losing twenty pounds - we found ourselves in Standard Three, which was in charge of a very popular teacher called Garner. His Christian name was Daniel and he was commonly known as 'Mucky Dan', though I never knew why, because he was always neat and clean in person. His great hobby was fishing, and on any fine summer evening he was to be found with his rod and line at the Big Pool. We seldom saw him catch anything, but we had unshakeable faith in his prowess and we always said that when he did catch one it would be a big 'un, and sure enough it was! On one occasion, fishing at a place a few miles from Runcorn, he actually caught a pike of record weight for the district, somewhere about twenty pounds if I remember rightly.

After this brief glance at the teachers, what of the pupils they had to teach? These were graded according to age, six years old in Standard One, seven in Standard Two, and so on. At the end of the school year in July, a boy whose progress had not been satisfactory could be 'kept down', but this happened only very rarely.

'Boat Children' must have been a serious problem for the Education Authorities. These were the children who lived on the 'flats' and barges that carried cargoes on the Bridgewater canal. When the boats were near a town loading and unloading for two or three days the children were sent to the nearest school, and often they came to ours. It is not surprising that their education suffered greatly. That was obvious enough even to us, because usually they could neither read nor work out the simplest sum.

However, boat children formed only a very small minority of my class mates. The bulk of them were from working class homes in the immediate district.

If somebody had made a casual visit to our classroom, his overriding impression would surely have been one of poverty. Some of us, perhaps

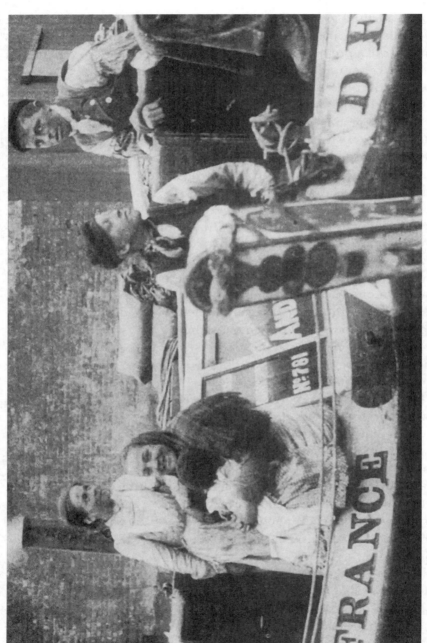

*Boat Children*

a quarter of the total, looked healthy, well-fed and decently clothed, but with the majority it was far otherwise. They looked half-starved and shabby, a proportion without shoes and stockings even in the harshest weather. Often they had sores on their faces, especially round their lips. In some cases too, their unwashed bodies and unwashed clothing made it positively unpleasant to be in their vicinity. Children are not commonly over-fastidious, but I well remember how unhappy some of us were if we found ourselves sitting next to one of these specially neglected children.

In the corresponding Girls' Department which my sisters attended, the presence of such children gave rise to another trouble which we boys with our short hair were spared. There was a constant spread of infestation from girls with dirty heads to girls with clean ones. Conscientious mothers managed to keep the problem to a minimum, but it could never be eliminated as long as the child remained at school. Nowadays, a number of factors including better economic conditions, the activities of the school nurse and the preference for shorter hair have all combined to put an end to this most offensive state of affairs.

But if on one hand attendance at a public elementary school was accompanied by some unpleasant features, on the other hand it was cheap. In the Infants' school we paid a penny a week and twopence in Standard One, and this rose in the course of two or three years to fourpence. In 1891 even these modest fees were abolished, and education became completely free.

No doubt many parents shrank from sending their children to a school where they might find themselves next to malodorous classmates and there were a number of fee-paying private schools. There would be higher standards of speech, but whether the standard of education was any better I have no means of knowing.

To return to the question of poverty at the school I attended, the following small incident illustrates it very clearly.

In July of 1957 I happened to be visiting Runcorn, and as I was walking along Halton Road one afternoon I was stopped by a man of my own age. It was evidently somebody who knew me, although I failed to recognise him. Then he introduced himself as Sam Rogers and I remembered him immediately, although we had not met since we both left the National School in 1895 or 1896. We had a most interesting talk over old times and then I remarked, "One thing strikes me very much, Sam. I hope you won't think me rude, but though you now look to me the picture of health, you didn't look so in the old days. Did you get enough to eat?"

"No I didn't, Walter," he said, and went on to give a few details. He was one of five children and his father, a labourer, earned only eighteen shillings a week. At noon on a Saturday, which was pay day, his mother would go out to meet her husband, for otherwise after a prolonged visit to the pub the eighteen shillings would be sadly depleted. To help out, Mrs Rogers used to take in washing.

With variations in point of detail, this scenario must have applied to a good number of the homes of my classmates, - large family, small income, and all too often the father a heavy drinker.

Just one other side-light on this subject of working class poverty. The winter of 1895-96 was one of exceptional severity. For weeks together the canal was frozen over, the ice being so thick that traffic was brought to a standstill and men were thrown out of work. One morning a strange gentleman walked into our classroom and, with the approval of the teacher, asked those boys who had had no breakfast that morning to put up their hands. Nearly a half did so. They were marched off somewhere and returned about twenty minutes later having been given, so they told us, a bowl of good hot soup and some bread. The rest of us wished that there was some other way of qualifying for this, other than having your father out of work.

I rarely pass a school playground at the time of the morning break without stopping to look at the children, particularly from the point of view of their physical well-being. With scarcely an exception they appear to be clean, healthy, well fed and warmly clad.

An account of schoolboys as I knew them sixty or seventy years ago would not be complete without some mention of fighting. Perhaps boys don't fight now, or we may have been a particularly quarrelsome lot, but certain it is that fights were common. The quarrel would start with a conversation something on the following lines:

A. "I've got my eye on you."

B. "Yes, and I've got my eye on you, too."

A. "I got the stick and you didn't, and you were talking just as much as I was."

B. "Well, teacher happened to see you and he didn't see me. That was just your bad luck."

A. "Yes, but you laughed when I got it."

B. "I didn't."

A. "You did."

B. "I didn't."

Now this sort of thing might go on indefinitely with no particular sequel. On the other hand A might suddenly declare, "Well, there's your cagent", giving B a light blow on the shoulder. (I can give no certain information as to the origin of this curious word, but it might have some connection with throwing down the 'gage', which was the knight's challenge to battle). The 'cagent' was also a challenge, and the surrounding boys rejoiced to see it because of the developments which might now be expected. B's choice was a simple one. He must either take up the challenge with a return blow, in which case the fight was 'on', or he must endure the ignominy of having refused to fight after receiving the cagent - an ignominy emphasised by the chanting of the surrounding group:

"Cowardy cowardy custard

Eat a lump of mustard."

There may be no more significance in the use of the word 'mustard' than that it rhymes easily with 'custard'. On the other hand, perhaps the suggestion is that a lump of that stimulating condiment might supply a sort of Dutch courage.

Once the fight had started, it was conducted in accordance with a few simple rules. The thumb had to be held touching, but outside of, the fingers of the clenched fist, not between the second and third fingers which would give a projecting thumb nail know as 'Coward's fist'. If you had the good fortune to knock your opponent down, you must not hit him again until he had regained his feet. If on the other hand you could hook your left arm round his neck and force his head downwards, you had achieved a very strong tactical position, and your backers were sure to exclaim: "Give it 'im under." With your right fist you could punch his imprisoned face for all you were worth. At any moment the fight would stop if one of the contestants shouted "Will you give in?" and the other agreed to do so. He retired perhaps with a bleeding nose, a black eye and a torn collar, but with honour untarnished.

Personally I hated being involved in a fight, and yet that was often my fate. If the cagent stage could no longer be warded off, I just did the best I could. For one thing I didn't like those personal references to 'custard' and 'mustard', and for another, my elder brother William had been a warrior of great note, and I felt there was a sort of family tradition to maintain.

Moreover, when we were both still at school, there was always the risk that he would take umbrage on my behalf. I well remember one occasion when we were on our way home together and I, being a man of peace, was taking a tactful line with a potential adversary. William joined in the discussion, and soon began to throw out dark hints of the fearful retribution that might be expected at my hands if apologies were not forthcoming. The more pointed William's hints became, the greater my alarm, but honour had to be upheld. I don't remember the outcome of that particular fight. Sometimes I won, and that might have been one of the occasions.

Should the battle be going against one there was still hope. A Mrs Bancroft kept a small shop close to our usual battle ground, and quite frequently she would sally forth with a wet dishcloth with which she would belabour both contestants quite impartially; or sometimes a teacher would pass by and put an end to the fight.

They say that Wellington at Waterloo exclaimed: "Would that night or Blucher would come!" With at least equal earnestness I have often wished that either Mrs Bancroft's dishcloth or a passing teacher would make a providential appearance.

All this might give the impression that at the National School we studied nothing but pugilistics, but this was far from being the case. We had a full programme of the more conventional subjects: the 'three R's', English, Scripture, Geography, Singing and Drawing. Our English course consisted chiefly of grammar and the writing of very simple 'compositions', while in each of the last three years we studied a play of Shakespeare. Much attention was paid to spelling and we had frequent exercises in dictation.

Perhaps because ours was a Church of England School, great prominence was given to Scripture and the Catechism. The first lesson of every day, except on Friday when we recited the Catechism, was devoted to Scripture, and before we left school at the age of twelve or thirteen, we had acquired a very good knowledge of all the 'story' parts of the Old Testament, and of the Gospels and the Acts of the Apostles. Each year, too, we had to learn a selected passage of Scripture, and as I recall some of them now: the Beatitudes, the parable of the Prodigal Son and that part of John XIV beginning 'let not your hearts be troubled', I think these were very well chosen.

As I recall it, the Scripture teaching was some of the best we had. For one thing it was mainly narrative, and stories are always acceptable to children.

Scripture, as I have said, was a bright spot, but in most other subjects the teaching was good only in so far as it consisted of 'drill'. As a result of much oral repetition we had a sound knowledge of our multiplication and other tables, lengths, weights and measures and so on, and this greatly helped us in arithmetic. Handwriting received careful attention and so did spelling and reading aloud. In geography much use was made of maps, and we acquired a good general knowledge of the position of countries, towns, important physical features and much other detailed knowledge obtainable through this medium.

But beyond the results that could be obtained through what I have called 'drill', nothing much. For one thing, nothing more seems to have been demanded by the Education Code of the day, but the main reason undoubtedly, was that with one or two exceptions, the teachers themselves were seriously lacking in culture. They were miserably paid, and the country got what it paid for.

With a well-stocked library and with teachers who knew and loved the books in it, a taste for good literature might have been developed, especially at a time when there were no counter-attractions in the shape of cinema, radio and television.

As it was, we acquired little more than the mechanical art of reading aloud. Even our compositions gave the least possible scope to the imagination. There was a limited variety of subjects, and animals were such a regular choice that we worked to a set formula: description - where found - habits - uses. The name of the animal must not be used more than once, and this taxed our ingenuity to the utmost as the stock of synonyms was not unlimited. Thus if the subject was 'The Bear', a few lines further down we could use 'Bruin', but if the composition ran to any length we were soon reduced to 'Old Grizzly' and 'This creature of the woods'. If we were dealing with birds, 'Our feathered friends' and 'These little songsters' would keep us going for a while.

In Geography, although we could point to places on the map, and recite the names of capes and rivers and bays in the correct order, we knew nothing of the pulsating life of peoples in other lands. Our drawing too was a very mechanical business. Instead of drawing and colouring objects that really interested us, such as boys making a snowman or a Red Indian peering out from behind a tree, we were taught simply the cold elements of the subject; how to draw straight lines, curved lines, cubes, and pyramids. In music the position was rather better, for we learnt a certain number of songs, but here again formal 'drill' was far too much in evidence, with the 'doh - me - soh - doh' of the modulator and the 'la - la - la - la' of the time exercise. To sum it up in one short word, it was all so *dull.*

How different is the state of affairs in a good school today! To give just one example, I visited a Junior School recently and watched a drawing lesson in progress. Each boy had a large sheet of paper on his desk, and as Christmas was approaching he was asked to make a picture of something appropriate to the season. He was allowed to get any inspiration he could from old Christmas cards, pictures and calendars. They were all soon so absorbed in the work that when the time came for morning break, the master had almost to drive them into the playground. I was much impressed with the high quality of their drawing and colouring, a consequence no doubt of the fact that they had enjoyed doing it.

They were encouraged to use any reasonable method to overcome difficulties. One boy for instance was not satisfied with his representation of a how a boy stands when he is sliding, so with the master's permission he got a friend to accompany him into the school yard, where he did some quick rough sketching while his friend posed. Here, what for us had been a dead subject, was brought to life.

I have quoted at length the example of drawing, but in most other subjects too there is a 'live' approach in present-day teaching, and the standard is far higher than it was in the 'nineties.

When I was at the National School there was no 'Eleven-Plus' in the modern sense, but somewhere about 1892 or 1893, the Cheshire Education Committee did start to offer a few scholarships. There were only twenty four for the whole County, and these were competed for by children of twelve or thirteen from the Seventh and ex-Seventh standards. They were tenable at what would now be called Grammar Schools, but as there was no such school in Runcorn at that time, any child who won a scholarship had to travel daily to a distant town, the nearest being the Verdin Grammar School at Winsford, which was twelve miles away. Travelling costs were included in the scholarship.

I saw no evidence of special examination pressure. We had some homework each night but only a little; some 'spellings' to learn or perhaps two or three sums to work out. We could usually do what was wanted in twenty minutes or so, leaving the rest of the evening available for play. Needless to say, we took full advantage of this state of affairs.

Today, although it is not officially approved, youngsters are being coached for the 'Eleven Plus'. Heavy pressure is being put on them by parents to improve their chances of gaining a place at a Grammar School, resulting all too often in harassed children and worried parents, with nothing at the end of it but disappointment for all of them.

The children of my day were spared this, but it has to be remembered that many who were highly intelligent never had the chance of a Grammar School education when so few scholarships were offered. Such children would now have a free passage through to University, probably to end up as professional men, whereas seventy years ago they more likely ended up as labourers.

Though in general the standard of culture amongst teachers was low, and their lessons dull and uninspiring on that account, our headmaster Mr Jordan was a shining exception, and in Standard Seven he taught us fairly frequently. He was born in or about the year 1840, and so could easily remember John Brown and Abraham Lincoln and the American Civil War. He remembered the Crimean War too, and told us tales of the winter of 1854-1855, when the cold was so intense that the men on getting up in the morning found their trousers frozen as stiff as boards, so that they could actually make them stand up. He would make an arithmetic lesson on stocks and shares 'come alive', by taking us in thought to the Stock Exchange and introducing us to 'bulls' and 'bears' and 'stags'. If only we had had a few more teachers with the same wide knowledge and interests, and the gift for communicating them!

**Standard VII, 1895**
*Walter is standing fourth from the right, second row.*

With teaching such as we received from him, discipline looked after itself and there was no need for punishment. Usually however, the connection between teaching and punishment was a very intimate one. It was once said in olden days that education was regarded as a mass of information that had somehow to be got inside the skin, and that the best way to get it there was frequent application of a cane *to* the skin. Certainly in my day the recipe was followed with great thoroughness. There were other punishments such as standing on a form for half an hour or more, but the cane was the teacher's great standby. I recall a simple but very typical example. We were in Standard Three so we must have been eight, and the teacher had asked a boy in the front row: "What is Oxford famous for?" He couldn't answer so he was given a vigorous stroke of the cane, applied diagonally across his back. Other boys in the row were asked the same question, one after another, none being missed, with the same result.

I was in the second row, and a swift count showed me that after three more boys in the front row and four in the second had been asked, it would by my turn, and certainly I had not the least idea of the answer. "What is Oxford famous for?" (whack). "What is Oxford famous for?" (whack)... and so it went on. The number of wriggling backs was rapidly increasing. Only three more boys and I was for it! How thankful I was that just at that point a boy answered: "University, sir. " Yes, that was it! I didn't know exactly what a University was, but Oxford was famous for it, and I have remembered that interesting fact ever since.

The cane was in constant use, usually with just a single stroke on the hand. Business was particularly brisk in arithmetic lessons, the procedure being very cut and dried. The sum was set on the blackboard, we worked it out on our slates, then changed with one another for marking. The correct answer was announced, and any boy with the sum wrong had to stand on the form and received one stroke - not a very hard one - with the cane. After this the round was repeated. Under these circumstances it will be clear that one's chances of going through a whole week without a single caning was very small indeed. My parents had made a standing offer of an extra penny for any week in which I could manage it.

Success would double my normal week's wages so I tried very hard indeed, but rarely achieved my reward. I so well remember one occasion when I very nearly did succeed. It was three thirty on Friday afternoon, and I had a clean sheet! The last lesson of the week, from three thirty to four fifteen, was one which we all enjoyed especially; community singing, I suppose it would be called today. Curtains between classes were drawn back, so that the complete schoolroom formed a sizeable hall. The various classes stood round the walls and we were free to 'mix up' if we wished, so I always stood next to my brother William. On this occasion I began by imparting the important information that this week I was alright for the special penny.

"Littler! Walter Littler I mean. Were you talking?"

"Yes, sir."

"Come here!"

It was my own class teacher, calling from the other side of the room. I went to him.

"Hold out your hand."

It was quite a light smack, but my penny was gone. It was awful!

In the ordinary way the caning was perfunctory and didn't hurt very much. No sense of disgrace was attached to it; no hard feelings on either side, one might almost say. But if the teacher were out of temper for the moment he could express his feelings by hitting hard, and that was quite another matter. I remember getting one such beating in Standard Six, at the age of eleven. It was the turn of the boy next to me to read aloud, the subject matter being a poem relating to some South African episode. I remember only the solitary line that was my undoing; 'And we came on the burghers lying'. . .

My neighbour stumbled over the unusual word 'burghers', getting only as far as "bur- bur-." I prompted him with a whispered "burglars", which he called out loudly. Everybody laughed except the teacher.

"What made you say 'burglars'?" he asked angrily.

"I - I - I don't quite know sir."

"Littler, did you whisper 'burglars'?"

"I might have done, sir."

"You might? You did, you mean! And you knew it wasn't really 'burglars', didn't you?"

. . . an uncomfortable pause.

"Well sir, I. . . "

"That's quite enough! Come here and hold out your hand!"

He gave only one stroke, but such a hard one that a weal resulted which was visible for at least a fortnight.

Following a caning that really hurt, there were certain permissible reactions. The sufferer might curl up his smarting hand and blow through it, as one sometimes sees workmen do on a frosty morning. If he felt much pain after three or four strokes, he might on reaching his desk hide his face in his curled-up arm. At this point teacher and class would be watching him to see if he wagged his head, for this was regarded as the running-up of the Jolly Roger. Vengeance was swift, the teacher descending upon him to administer some really hard cuts across the shoulder.

Playing truant or 'wagging it' was a very serious offence, serious for parents because it was punishable at law, and serious for pupils because they automatically received a severe caning from Mr Jordan.

We had two School Attendance Officers in Runcorn, for some mysterious reason known as 'Cockies'. They were 'Cocky' Bowyer and 'Cocky' Howard, and they pursued their calling so diligently through so many years that the title became hereditary and was applied to anybody who happened to have the same surname. The 'habitual truant' was a species unknown in the Runcorn of the 'nineties.

If with most of our teachers caning for minor offences was a fairly perfunctory affair, this was far from being the case with Bill Slasher in Standard Five. He was like a character out of Dickens, except that Mr Wackford Squeers would have seemed mild and enlightened by comparison.

We had an introduction to him at any early date, for when we were seven and in Standard Two, we were at one end of the long schoolroom with Standard Five in the middle. There was not even a curtain between us.

We used to watch the proceedings with fascinated gaze. The canings were so hard and so frequent that I have often wondered since that he wasn't prosecuted for assault. These days he certainly would be. Sometimes when we talked to the bigger boys about caning they would say: "Caning? You kids don't know what it is! Wait till you get into Slasher's class!" This horrible doom drew relentlessly nearer, but to our immense relief Slasher left about a year before he would have been teaching us. He was a brute, as typical of the worst sort of teacher as Mr Jordan was of the best.

*'Cocky' Howard, photographed with his wife, Mary.*

The fact that we were able to witness Slasher's activities underlines an important point, that classes were not properly separated. We had only two rooms that were satisfactory in this respect. They were known as 'top' and 'bottom' classrooms, for Standards One and Six respectively. Standard Seven was curtained off and had reasonable privacy.

The remaining four classes were all accommodated in the big schoolroom, divided along most of its length by a wall, with a gap at the end covered by a curtain. The headmaster's desk stood by this - he had no room of his own - and for morning and evening prayers it was drawn back so that he could see all five classes. This meant that there were two classes on either side of the wall that had no division of any sort.

This plan, with minor variations, was in essence the old village schoolroom, and buildings of the same type are still to be found lingering on, a hundred years out of date, in every town and city of the land.

After I had been about three years at the school, curtains were fixed between the two classes on either side of the wall, and before I left these were replaced by sliding wooden screens which provided us with really effective separation.

Not only was there no headmaster's room; there was no staff room either. Sanitary arrangements were barely adequate and there was only a solitary cracked washbasin, used in emergencies when a cut or a case of nose bleeding had to be dealt with.

Another very unsatisfactory feature of the schools of this period was the size of the classes. Usually there was sixty or seventy boys in each, except in Standard Seven when they were on the constant lookout for jobs and leaving as they secured them.

This is no doubt why talking was always regarded as a punishable offence. The alternative was hubbub. This too may be the reason why we never asked the teacher a question. To give just one example. We were taught in Standard Five that Astrakhan on the Caspian Sea was noted for caviar, shagreen and isinglass. I don't think any of us knew what these things were and it certainly didn't occur to any of us to enquire, so questions were probably discouraged. Lively questioning from sixty or seventy children would inevitably have involved noise, and noise was 'Public Enemy Number One'.

Present day classes are of course much smaller. They rarely exceed forty five and the average is only thirty eight. Even these figures are regarded as nothing short of a public scandal, but so far have we progressed in seventy years that the elementary teachers of my schooldays would have hailed classes of forty five as the New Jerusalem.

Now to return to that strange character Bill Slasher, or rather to the class of teacher he represented. Though none of our other teachers could compete with him in the vigour and frequency with which he wielded the cane, there was a Mr Tanwell who wasn't far behind. My brother William had to put up with him for a year, and showed certain points of resemblance to:

'Some village Hampden that with dauntless breast
The little tyrant of his fields withstood'.

Open warfare would have been suicidal, but William was very successful with what would now be called a Cold War. One day for instance Tanwell snapped out, "You're not attending, Littler. Keep your eyes on me!" William obeyed at once. When Tanwell moved, the eyes were still upon him. Rather uneasily, he walked to the other side of the class, but still could not escape that fixed gaze. It was a modern reproduction of Wedding Guest v. Ancient Mariner.

Finally Tanwell's patience ran out - he had no great stock of it - and he burst out with: "Take your eyes off me, Littler!" Beginning with a respectful "Please sir," the Ancient Mariner explained pathetically that he just didn't know what to do. He had only just been trying to obey the earlier injunction "Keep your eyes on me," and now he was in trouble again!

But Tanwell saved it up for him, and a day or two later, for some quite trivial offence, gave him such a severe beating that father decided to intervene. It was then that he learned of the incident just related, and a few others. I am not certain that he didn't feel a certain sympathy for Tanwell!

After father's protest there was some improvement, but there was no real peace until the end of July came and William left school for good. He was not quite thirteen.

To conclude this chapter with a general survey, it can be said that though the cane was used much more frequently than was usual in such schools, the situation was not as bad as it sounds. Caning was for the most part such a nominal affair that we didn't think much about it and certainly felt no sense of injustice.

Teaching was good in so far as it was a matter of routine exercises, but it lacked the life and variety that only teachers of better education and wider outlook themselves could have given it. But to have asked in those days for anything more would have been to ask for the moon. Neither the equipment - books, projectors, a gymnasium and so forth - nor the human material were available. Our school was probably as good as most others and a great deal better than many, and for my own part I am more inclined to be thankful for what it achieved, than to condemn it for failing to attain the impossible.

We were indeed fortunate in having a headmaster both well-informed and of impressive personality. I have spoken of his teaching, but my most abiding memory of him is associated with our assembly for dismissal at the end of the day. We have sung our evening hymn: 'Glory my God to Thee this night'. There is perfect stillness. At the end of the long room we see an ageing man, his silvery head bowed, and then he speaks the opening words of Cranmer's lovely prayer, "Lighten our darkness we beseech Thee oh Lord...," and somehow the dingy old schoolroom has taken on a strange beauty.

# CHAPTER 6

# Religious and Moral Training

In the preceding two chapters I have described the education I received at an elementary school, and this must have been typical of thousands of others of the same period.

Of equal or greater importance was the training I received at home. If this training had been special or peculiar, a description of it would not be of much value, but it was in fact characteristic of a large section of the community. Those of the lower-middle and working classes where Methodism had a particularly strong hold were striving, God-fearing men and women, their lives in some respects rather narrow and rigid, but founded on principle and in sharp contrast to those who through their feckless and degraded existence had sunk still lower in the social scale.

They could be said to have formed a class of their own; the backbone of Victorian England which, with the decline of religious faith, the rising tide of material prosperity and the wide variety of leisure activities now available to all, has disappeared for ever.

I have used the word 'training' for want of a better, but since home environment played just as great a part as the conscious efforts of my parents to bring us up in the right way, perhaps 'influence' would be more appropriate.

It is hardly possible to write about religious and moral influence without including some description of those who are exerting it, in this case my parents; and so I must add a little to what has already been said of them earlier on.

Both were sincere Christians of the evangelical sort, but they were of two quite distinct types. Mother was attuned by nature to a sense of Christian values; to a capacity for self-sacrifice and obedience to the Will of God.

Father, in the first instance, could have been described as the 'commercial' type of Christian. When he entered upon the Christian life - as he did shortly before his marriage and largely as a result of mother's influence - it is probable that he regarded it in the light of a 'contract' or 'covenant'. As the little stories of his boyhood show, belief in a literal heaven and hell was very intense in his day, and in the humble circles in which he moved. His 'contract' secured him for the future, but on the other hand it called for much inconvenient sacrifice on his part. He must give freely; he must 'visit the widowed and the fatherless in their affliction', he must allow Christian values to have first place in his life.

A little way back I used the words 'in the first instance' and they are important, for what to begin with seemed a set of rather grim obligations, developed into a way of life that he felt was worth living for its own sake. Of course this way of life didn't come as easily to him as to my mother, but he worked hard at it and achieved much, even if he didn't scale the spiritual heights.

In my childhood days, the commercial type of Christian was very common indeed. This arose from the fact that the rewards and punishments attending the religious life - as these rewards and punishments were then understood - were very clear and tangible. It followed that the man with a business mind regarded the adoption of Christianity as a sort of long-term investment which could be expected to yield excellent returns. Usually his favourite text was 'Godliness is profitable unto all things, having promise of the life that now is, and of that which is to come'.

Many like my father, having entered upon the Christian life for 'commercial' reasons, continued to live it because more and more they realised its moral value. But there were others who never progressed beyond the stage of the business deal, and all too often they cheated!

I remember one who could be vulgarly described as a 'regular twister' who attached great importance to the fact that he never shaved on Sundays! Another example is the Mr Sandford mentioned in an earlier chapter, who was also very insistent on Sunday observance, but who starved his servants and made promises he never intended to keep.

The kind of religious training I should receive from such parents as I have described is self-evident. We were taught to say a simple prayer from a very early age, and the Bible was always a prominent element.

Mother would tell us stories from it when we were very young, but as we grew older my brother William and I read aloud from it every night, mother sitting by to help us with the hard words. To encourage bible-reading at other times I am afraid she was not above adding the attractions of filthy lucre, quoting a somewhat obscure passage and offering a prize of a halfpenny to the one who should find it first.

We were taught to regard the Bible as true in every detail. This was easy enough in childhood, but as I grew older and my horizons enlarged I ran into difficulties. This must have been an experience common to many at that period of rapid scientific advancement, and I will give some account later on of how I was able at last to reconcile the old beliefs and teaching with the new knowledge.

Of Sunday, I will say no more now than that we were taught to observe it as a Holy Day. This observance however was kept within reasonable limits and we didn't find it irksome.

So much for our religious background. Moral training is not necessarily a separate thing, but good parents would try to instil into their children certain moral principles, even if they were not themselves religious.

The first moral quality I had to learn - or be helped to learn - was common honesty. Like any other very young child I had no natural sense of right or wrong as regards theft. Two of my very earliest memories when I was about four years old illustrate this point.

First, I remember standing outside a grocer's shop where some of the goods, including eggs, were displayed on a wooden stall projecting over the pavement. I paused for some time, considering whether to take two of the eggs and run away with them. Finally I desisted, deciding that it was too risky, but it never occurred to me that it was wrong.

Shortly afterwards I was walking along Rutland Street with my sister Nellie, then about thirteen. We were approaching a sweet shop kept by a Mrs Shaw, and I announced that I was going to buy a ha'porth of jelly babies. "Alright," said Nellie, "but I didn't know you had a halfpenny." I hadn't, but my plans were all laid.

We went into the shop and the jelly babies, wrapped in paper, were quickly supplied. I seized the little packet and was out of the shop in a few seconds. I could hear loud, startled exclamations from behind me, but of course had no time to enter into a discussion. The pursuit was on!

I could easily have outdistanced Mrs Shaw, who suffered from the double handicap of stoutness and having to make her way round the counter. With Nellie it was another matter. I was soon overtaken and obliged to surrender my precious packet. I have no memory whatever of the sequel. Nellie would have informed mother, who would not have found it necessary to do more than explain that taking something that didn't belong to you was wrong, and so a conscience in the matter of stealing would be born.

Such a parental reaction would seem so obvious as to be scarcely worth a mention, but with dishonesty so widespread, how many parents one wonders 'turn a blind eye', or worse still commend the child for its smartness? So the first step is taken along the road that leads to a first appearance in a Children's Court.

Of all the deadly sins, lying was looked upon as the deadliest. I have heard my father say that if he had told a lie, his father would have thrashed him within an inch of his life. This is one of the very few things I ever heard about my paternal grandfather, and it seems an odd contradiction on the part of a man who died in a drunken stupor in a field, that he should proceed to such extremes when a child of something less than seven told a lie. Yet there is logic behind it. Truth, its opposite, is a cardinal virtue. In the literal meaning of the word, all morality hinges upon it. One cannot stray far down the path of transgression without meeting it face to face.

Being 'found out in a lie' is still one of my most painful childhood memories. It was a double offence because I had told it in an attempt to cover up an act of disobedience. I was so overwhelmed by the shame of what I had done that I received no other punishment, and indeed I needed none. A morbid 'guilt complex' hung over me like a black cloud for months.

I had one character flaw which is by no means common to all children and that was a violent temper. Often this was called forth by the teasing of older brothers, and I well remember one occasion at the age of about eight when I became fiercely enraged with two of them; William who was eleven, and Charlie, seventeen. I seized a cube-shaped tin of Vaseline weighing about a pound, and holding it in both hands, hurled it with all my strength at Charlie. The edge of it struck him on the shin, leaving what turned out to be a very nasty bruise and cut. The sequel was a matter of seconds. While Charlie was nursing his shin, William advanced to do battle, but when I snatched up a bread knife he bolted, with me in hot pursuit. Fortunately I did not catch him.

Maybe if I had done I would not have used the knife. I hope not, but I don't know. At any rate, here was obviously a very serious state of affairs and mother was much troubled about it. She pointed out that a strong person could control his temper; it was only a weak one who could not. Naturally the Bible was quoted: 'He that ruleth his spirit is better than he that taketh a city'. She explained that 'taking a city' is doing something outside yourself, while 'ruling the spirit' is doing something inside, and a far harder thing.

Again, I received no punishment. I suppose she saw that she had really persuaded me to do my very best in this great matter of 'ruling the spirit', and that being the case, punishment would be worse than useless. I had many a failure, most of them in connection with games of draughts! I often played this game with William, and with an age difference of three and a half years he would win at least two games out of three. I would make a bad move, realising this just after I had 'taken my hands off'. Had he seen it? Yes, - I could see by the little grin of anticipation playing round his lips. Then came the great struggle. My inclination was to sweep all the pieces from the board and very often that was what I did. But now and then, and with gradually increasing frequency, I managed to 'rule the spirit'.

In time the violent outbursts ceased altogether. Increasing age would be helping me in any case, but my mother's wise treatment of me and my desire not to disappoint her were much more potent factors.

In one respect at least, my parents conformed to the most up-to-date concepts of child training. If there ever was any disagreement between them as to how a particular offence was to be dealt with, it was thrashed out in private and we never knew of it. To the children they presented a united front. As for the punishments themselves, theirs was not the doctrine of 'spare the rod and spoil the child'. We were smacked or whipped on occasion. Father had a piece of rope known as 'the gingerbread' for which we had a healthy respect, but other punishments were preferred, and often we weren't punished at all.

There was however one aspect of our home training that left much to be desired.  Mother was in many ways enlightened and ahead of her times, but in common with most women of her day she took no steps to see that we had necessary and suitable sex instruction.  That perhaps would have been father's business as far as we boys were concerned, but I am sure he would have followed her suggestions if she had given a lead.  As a result we grew up feeling there was something not only mysterious but positively wicked about this aspect of human life.

Our home was not peculiar in this respect.  The attitude was general, and often disastrous.  Many young girls 'got into trouble' out of sheer ignorance.  Meanwhile others, many still in their teens, entered lightly and innocently into marriage, all too often with appalling psychological consequences.

Most parents today have a much more enlightened approach, but many still find it a difficult subject to discuss with their children.  The alternative is usually the passing of hole-and-corner misinformation from one child to another, and because this undoubtedly still takes place there is much to be said for formal sex instruction in schools, at any rate for those parents who would prefer it.

We hear more and more these days about 'rights'.  Where children are concerned it's their right to good housing, a balanced diet, a sound education.  Of course they should have all these things and one can only rejoice that their general standard of physical well-being has improved so greatly through most of this century.  But too often they are being denied the greatest right of all - in prosperous homes as much as in poor ones - and that is their right to a sound moral upbringing which will nourish and sustain them as long as their lives shall last.

**St. Paul's Methodist Church, 1966 - 1969**
*Nicklaus Pevsner in his 'Buildings of Britain' describes its demolition as the loss of the only distinctive feature in Runcorn's town centre.*

# CHAPTER 7

# Church and Sunday School

If anybody were to take a walk round Runcorn at Church time on a Sunday morning, and he were old enough to remember taking a similar walk round about 1890, he would be impressed by one remarkable difference. In 1890 he would have seen an astonishing number of people trooping to church or to one of the corresponding nonconformist 'chapels'. Greenway Road for instance would be filled with a lively procession, not so much of individuals as of families. There would be Father in his silk hat and frock coat, accompanied by his wife and perhaps three or four children, for families were larger in those days and four was really quite a modest number.

There were of course no motor cars, but a few of the wealthier families would be in their carriages drawn by one or even two horses.

Today the one-time lively procession has dwindled to a mere trickle, and places of worship which were once comfortably filled are many of them almost empty with the few remaining 'regulars' - for some unexplained reason - usually huddled at the back. This falling-off is especially marked in the chapels; rather less so in the churches.

In the earlier period in fact attendance at a place of worship was 'The Thing'. It was hardly respectable *not* to attend, apart from the fact that many of those who went were influenced by religious motives. Amongst the working classes the proportion of church or chapel goers was probably not quite so high, though much higher than would be the case today.

The doctrinal differences between church and chapel were not really very great, but they were accompanied by certain other differences. The churchman was usually a Conservative, the nonconformist a Liberal. The churchman was more tolerant on such matters as moderate drinking, dancing, theatre-going and card-playing. Most nonconformists were total abstainers and would have nothing to do with any of these pastimes, which were looked upon as Works of the Devil. This summary would be much less true today. Politically the Labour Party has drawn large numbers from both groups, and the typical nonconformist no longer objects to dancing or the theatre. In many cases though he remains teetotal, and although he enjoys a game of cards he doesn't play for money.

To those not familiar with the origin of 'Chapel' as distinct from 'Church', it must be explained that 'Chapel' did not refer to a single institution comparable with the Church of England.

Then as now, there were innumerable sects which all came under the heading of 'nonconformist'. Of these, the Methodists formed easily the biggest single group, exerting great influence on late Victorian Society. They in their turn subdivided, though the Wesleyan Methodists could be regarded as the 'Mother Church' with various offshoots: the Primitive Methodists, the United Methodist Free Church and one or two still smaller ones. These recombined in 1932 to form the present-day Methodist Church; but they were all flourishing as separate entities in 1890.

Their common foundation lay in the religious experience of John Wesley and the great religious revival which he inspired, but there was never any doctrinal difference separating it from the Church of England such as divides the Protestant and Catholic religions. John Wesley himself and his brother Charles were the sons of an Anglican priest and never left the Church of England. It was only after John's death in 1792 that the movement towards separation became too strong to be resisted and 'The people called Methodists' formed themselves into an independent church with their own ministers.

Though in its fundamental and long lasting impact on society there could be no comparison, it was in effect a gigantic revivalist campaign and had points in common with that associated recently with Billy Graham.

In both cases the emphasis was on 'Conversion'. Thousands flocked to huge open-air meetings. Men came forward to the penitent forms in droves, and - another point of comparison - they were allocated to local churches.

But many of the eighteenth century clergy were idle and worse, and Wesley felt that his converts lacked the pastoral care they needed. So he formed them into 'classes' with about a dozen members in each, and a man of approved religious character was appointed 'Class Leader'. A number of classes would be grouped together to form a 'Society'.

A class would meet weekly, and each member in turn was expected to give some account of his spiritual experiences since the last meeting; his temptations and how he had met them; whether he had spoken to his fellow workmen on spiritual matters, and so on.

Wesley spent much of his life on horseback, travelling the length and breadth of the land to visit his 'Societies' and see that there was no straying from the fold. One entry in his journal throws an interesting sidelight on the buying and selling of smuggled or 'run' goods which was widespread in the eighteenth century:

"In the evening I preached at Sunderland. I then met the Society, and told them plain that none could stay with us unless he would part with all of his sin - particularly robbing the King, selling or buying run goods, which I could no more suffer than robbing on the highway. This I enforced on every member the next day. A few would not promise to refrain, so these I was forced to cut off. About 250 were of a better mind."

There must have been many a struggle between greed and conscience in the Cornish fishing villages, strongholds alike of smuggling and Methodism!

By my time the Methodist classes had not only 'held their own'; they had extended their range to include young people, and at the age of nine I was a member of a class that met on Wednesday evening, and so was my brother William who would be twelve at the time. On one never-to-be-forgotten occasion he had been pressurised into going and was not in a spiritual mood.

Ordinarily we had simply two or three hymns, a prayer and a Bible lesson, but this particularly evening we were 'met for tickets' by the superintendent minister, the Rev Thomas Wilkes. He explained the origin of Society classes, and especially explained how members gave their spiritual experiences of the preceding week. He gave examples of short, typical 'experiences' and, beginning with the older boys, invited us to give ours!

Strangely, so it seems to me now, he obtained a number of results. They ran very much to a pattern, usually something like "I have certainly had my temptations this week, but I am glad to say that with the help of

God I have been able to overcome them". Then - exciting moment! - he nodded to my brother.

"Let me see, you are William Littler aren't you? Would you like to give us your experience?"

To which William replied:

"Yes Sir, but it is only a very short experience because I haven't had any temptations."

Mr Wilkes: "Come my lad, we all have temptations. Just think a moment!"

William: (after a pause) "No Sir, I can't think of a single one."

Mr Wilkes: "Have you never been tempted to tell a lie?"

William: "No Sir, I never am much tempted that way." (This was probably the case. He was very truthful).

Mr Wilkes: "Have you never grumbled when your mother wanted you to run an errand?"

William: (Screwing up his face in what appeared to be an effort of recollection) "She hasn't asked me to run any this week."

Mr Wilkes: (getting rather to the bottom of his list) "What about fighting?"

William: "Well Sir, I did have a fight, but that was last week, not this."

At about this point Mr Wilkes desisted, clearly puzzled that Satan should have granted a whole week's immunity to such a promising young limb.

Revival meetings were a prominent feature of Methodist church life in the 1890's. They had the same object of securing conversions and usually lasted a week. A minister with special experience in such work would be engaged, of whom incidentally Gypsy Smith was one of the most famous, and the normal congregation would hold prayer meetings for some time before the great event. At the actual service, the sermon in particular was directed towards persuading the listener to come to the penitent form. In a successful series the converts might run into hundreds, and these would be allocated to various Society classes.

Usually only a very small proportion continued their membership for any length of time, though even a handful of genuine conversions would be felt to justify the missions.

They performed a valuable service insofar as they were able to reform straightforward 'drunks' and wife beaters of whom there were plenty, but unfortunately they had another and more sinister side to them. They resulted from time to time in cases of religious dementia, and I knew myself of two women in Runcorn who never completely recovered their mental stability after attending a series of these meetings.

I have a vivid recollection of a revival service I attended in Runcorn in or about the year 1900. This was a single service, not one of a series, and was held at the Salvation Army Citadel which was then located in High Street. The preacher was General William Booth, founder of the Salvation Army. He was then seventy one, and I thought that if I did not seize this chance of hearing him I might never have another. On the other hand, I had to sit for an important examination in a few weeks' time, and could ill spare an evening. Finally I decided to compromise. I would attend the service, but leave quietly when the General had finished his sermon.

For nearly an hour he preached with wonderful vigour and eloquence from the text 'What shall it profit a man if he gain the whole world and lose his own soul?' During the last few minutes he made an impassioned plea for any unconverted members of the congregation to come to the penitent form.

I was very glad to have seen and heard such a famous old man "and now", I thought, "I will just slip out quietly". There were difficulties! By coming in good time I had secured a seat quite near the platform, but a long way from the door of the hall, and part of the gangway space was packed with people. At best, 'slipping out' would have been a tedious process, but the real difficulty was the penitents.

A glance round showed me that as soon as a man or woman stood up, it was taken as a sign that he or she wished to go to the penitent form. Salvation Army officers and 'soldiers' were posted everywhere, and within seconds two of them would reach the penitent and bear him away, to the accompaniment of ecstatic exclamations: "Another soul for the Lord! Another brand plucked from the burning!"

I pondered the problem. I couldn't get out without first standing up. I couldn't stand up without being affectionately but firmly seized upon by a couple of stalwart Salvationists. I could of course have explained the situation to them, but felt very reluctant to hurt their feelings. Besides, if I did explain and make a start, during my slow progress to the door I should have to repeat my explanation to successive pairs of Salvationists. No, it was too painful, and I decided it was better on the whole to remain seated. But it was more than an hour before it was possible to make a move without the risk of misunderstandings.

An account of the church-going habits of my youth would not be complete without some reference to 'Sunday clothes'. Attendance at a place of worship had as its corollary the solemn joy of getting there and the processional route, especially in the morning, was always regarded as something in the nature of a fashion parade. A parade implies an audience, and this was not lacking, albeit discreet and largely invisible.

Not everybody could go to morning service, even in those days of greater piety. There were dinners to be cooked, and children and old people to be cared for. But there were compensations, for those with houses appropriately situated. If Mrs Smith had on a new hat, or the two eldest Miss Browns were turning out with a slightly heightened consciousness and quarter-yard trains to their new dresses, a hundred pairs of eyes would duly remark the fact. Mrs Smith and the Miss Browns would be fully aware of this hidden appraisal, although it would have taken an acute observer to detect the occasional twitch of a lace curtain as they passed on their way.

Strangely, this tradition of dressing up for Sunday was common to all classes. Even in the poorest families a new white frock was usually contrived for the eldest little girl, timed to make its first appearance on Whit Sunday morning. Last year's was passed on to the next in age, and so on down the line of sisters.

Best clothes even had an economic significance. In those days when pawnbrokers flourished and fattened everywhere on the half starved body of the British working class, it was quite a common practice for the housewife to pawn them on Monday morning and redeem them on Saturday night.

Some years later I had a friend living in 'digs' or 'lodgings' as we used to call them then, who fell victim to an extension of this principle. He was going home for a week's holiday, and wishing to 'travel light' he took only essentials in the way of clothing. However, he found when he got home that he was going to need his best suit after all, and as the distance was only ten miles or so he decided to go back and fetch it. He opened the wardrobe door expectantly, and was completely baffled to find the trousers of the suit missing. Enquiries were set on foot and it

***Small Holt Relative (identity uncertain) in Sunday Best***
*Both boys and girls were dressed in petticoats up to about five years of age.*

turned out that the landlady had pawned them, not expecting him to return until the end of the holiday.

Although all children from homes like ours went to chapel at least once and sometimes twice every Sunday, it was 'Sunday school' which played a much bigger part in our lives. Not, I regret to say that we found the afternoon service itself particularly stimulating, but because incidentally it provided us with the only social life we ever had.

Sunday schools have quite an interesting history, and may fairly be regarded as the foundation of our free educational system.

They really were schools to start with, held on a Sunday because even quite small children had to work and Sunday was their only free day.

They were started in 1790 by Robert Raikes, a well-to-do printer in Gloucester. He was distressed by the condition and behaviour of children in the streets 'so horrid as to convey to a serious mind an idea of hell rather than of any other place'.

He secured the services of four women who kept Dame Schools, and each being paid a shilling for their Sunday's work they were to teach the children to read, which was essential if they were to be able to read the Bible.

The movement spread rapidly to other towns, and it was estimated that within ten years there were three hundred thousand children in attendance.

Gradually payment ceased to be necessary as public-spirited people came forward and offered to teach for nothing.

As day schools increased in number, Sunday schools ceased to be needed for their original purpose, but they continued to be used for simple services including Bible lessons suitable for children, and there were also adult classes for young men and women.

Much later, a decline really did set in. Between 1887 and 1958 there has been a fall in attendance of nearly sixty per cent. This no doubt reflects the growing popular indifference to organised religion, but the advent of the family car has played its part as well. The family all go off for the day together, instead of weary parents enjoying an hour's rest after dinner while the children are packed off to Sunday school.

The one we Littlers attended in Lowland Road was known as Camden. It was not the oldest in town, but it did have the distinction of being the first Methodist chapel which Thomas Hazlehurst, a local soap manufacturer and philanthropist, built in Runcorn. Methodism in the

*William Holt, from a painting circa 1820*

area actually dated back to the 1780's, and my wife's great grandfather William Holt was a co-founder of Brumswick which was the very first Sunday school in 1800.

As a local preacher he did much to pioneer total abstinence and once, on the occasion of Hale Wakes, it landed him in gaol.

Hale was a small village on the outskirts of Widnes, and Wakes Day, when heavy drinking accompanied 'all the fun of the fair', was held on a certain Sunday each year. The local constable, himself a Methodist, brought this to William's attention, whereupon he and a friend decided to attend.

Their public denunciation of this desecration of the Sabbath led to an unseemly brawl and the local squire, to whom Dissenters were little better than heathen, ordered the self same constable to arrest and gaol them for causing an affray.

Tempers having cooled, the squire thought he had better let them out, but William, intent upon martyrdom, refused to *be* let out except by the squire in person, and in the end this was what the squire was obliged to do.

But to return to Camden. It was well placed, being on the edge of a large working class district, and the usual Sunday afternoon attendance was about three hundred. The proceedings were typical of all Sunday schools and remain substantially unaltered to this day. We began with a hymn and a prayer in the general assembly hall. After a second hymn we broke up into small classes each with its own teacher, meeting in separate vestries. We had a Bible lesson lasting for perhaps twenty minutes, then the classes reunited in the assembly hall for a final hymn and prayer.

The weak spot was the teaching, and Camden was probably not peculiar in this respect. If lively youngsters are to be kept quiet and attentive for even twenty minutes good teaching is essential, and there were not enough competent people available. The result was boredom, and boredom soon led to disorder. Well meaning, but hopelessly inadequate teachers were unmercifully ragged and the victims of practical jokes.

On one occasion a boy in my group split open a sausage and moulded the greasy contents round the vestry doorknob. When this was seized by the unsuspecting teacher as he entered, his language was the reverse of what might have been expected from one dedicated in theory to principles of moderation and restraint!

At the age of about nine my teacher reported me to an older brother for bad behaviour, and he duly carried the message to my parents. "All right my lad," father said, "next week you'll come with me to *my* Sunday school, and we'll see if you misbehave there!"

On the whole I was quite pleased. It would be a change, and interesting to see what Father's Sunday school was like. On the other hand - yes - I had certainly noticed a sort of threatening glint in his eye when he said "*my* Sunday school," and I wasn't altogether easy.

When we got there, there was a gentleman seated at a little desk in the middle of the room. Father addressed him as Brother Higgins. I rather liked the look of Brother Higgins. He would be sixty or so, and I thought he had a kind face. There were two or three others sitting on some benches, and a few drifted in until there would be about ten in all. It seemed they were all brothers. I think father must have told them I was coming because they didn't ask any questions.

Soon father's 'Sunday school' began. I now know it was not a 'Society' class, but a prayer meeting. We began with a hymn. That was alright, but rather short. Then the leader (Brother Higgins) said: "Brother Millinger will now lead us in prayer. "

Brother Millinger did. He led us for a long time. The floor was hard and I wanted to wriggle, but remembering what father had said about settling accounts when we got home if I misbehaved in the smallest particular, I managed to keep still. The prayer ended at last, and Brother Higgins said "Now let us have a verse of 'Sometimes a light surprises'. " That was better. We stood up and sang the verse - alas only one - and the leader said: "Brother Anderson will now lead us in prayer. "

We knelt again. It seemed to me that Brother Anderson was trying to outclass Brother Millinger in the matter of length, and that would have been no light achievement. Another verse of Cowper's hymn followed, then Brother Ward, and then another verse and so on. There were only four verses to the hymn, and my spirits rose. With all the verses used up it seemed the logical thing to do was to go home. But hopes were soon dashed. What did happen was that Brother Higgins gave a little Bible lesson. After this they sang the first verse of another hymn, and the remaining Brothers, including my father, were called upon one by one to lead us in prayer, one verse of the new hymn coming after each had taken his turn. It was an awful experience, lasting at least an hour and a half. The prayers were so long and the verses so short!

I don't know how those old fellows stood it. Certainly I never wanted to go to father's 'Sunday school' again.

The great day in the Sunday school year was the Anniversary, and ours was usually held in April. This called for special vocal efforts, and for several weeks before we would be practising the new songs under our conductor Mr Sam Bazley, a wonderful natural musician. Sam was not a product of an Academy or a Conservatoire. He was in fact a cobbler, and his little shop was just opposite Camden. I doubt whether he sold the 1890 version of the stiletto heel; he probably didn't sell shoes of any sort, but I remember the little card always displayed in his window: 'Rough lads well leathered'.

Camden was much too small for the Anniversary services. They took place in St. Paul's Methodist Chapel, another gift of the philanthropist Thomas Hazlehurst. It was a magnificent building, erected in 1866 and seating fifteen hundred people. Despite its size, the congregation was so large and so regular in attendance that families rented their pews! For those who wished to worship God but couldn't otherwise afford it, a few free pews were provided. These were below the gallery and to one side of the pulpit. However, for the Anniversary services all rights were waived and it was first come first served.

It was said of Sam that he never left Lowland Road except on this one day in the year when he walked to St. Paul's less than a quarter of a mile away, and I can well believe it was true. Camden and his cobbler's shop were his whole world; he wanted no other.

At the start of rehearsals he would rap his little stick on the desk and we all became quiet. "We'll begin with 'earts is little gardins'," he would say, and we had no difficulty in understanding that 'Hearts are little gardens' was intended. We received various exhortations from time to time such as "now yay basses!" (always a most vigorous response to this). We were not so successful when he asked for *'pianissimo'*. In fact I have heard him express the gloomy conclusion after years and years of experience, that "Ye can't larn Camden two p's."

However, in spite of Camden's limitations in this and other respects, he got his highly irregular choir into wonderful shape by the time the Anniversary came round. North country people have a natural love of

*Camden Sunday School*

singing, and apart from those of us who just enjoyed it, there were a few who were really gifted.

Two sisters in our choir had magnificent voices and Jenny's especially was outstanding, so much so that Philip Speakman who had made a fortune in the 'carrying trade' on the Bridgewater canal offered to have her professionally trained. He was convinced she had a great future before her and went full of enthusiasm to discuss his plans with her father. But Joe after listening in silence had only one comment to make: "She can go to t'wash tub, same as 'er mother."

A pathetic little tale, and often enough told I daresay in an age when waste of talent was as common and as tragic as waste of life itself. A novelist could perhaps make it a basis for a story, but a story requires an artistic ending and the truth is seldom artistic. Away to the washtub Jenny went, where she appeared to be perfectly happy, finding fresh fields for her vocal powers in the ordering of a numerous progeny.

But to return to the Anniversary. The day came at last for Sam to make his annual pilgrimage, though not as conductor of his own choir. The St Paul's choir master 'took over' at this point, and Sam sat with the congregation. He would listen critically, perhaps shaking his head a little gloomily when one of the quieter passages was being sung.

The great chapel was comfortably filled in the morning, but if you wanted a good seat in the evening you had to be there at least twenty minutes before the time announced for service, which was six o'clock. At about a quarter to, stewards began putting seats in the aisles, and in any other place where there was a tiny bit of room to spare. Soon afterwards the packed congregation stood to sing 'All people that on earth do dwell' to that majestic tune 'Old Hundredth', and another memorable service had begun.

Anniversary sermons were always of first class quality because only an outstanding preacher would be invited, and further, on an occasional visit such as this he would select one of his best sermons. Should he make a return visit on a subsequent occasion he had of course to be careful not to preach the same one again.

I remember this happening once, with a sort of dramatic rendering of the Twenty-third Psalm. After reading the first line or two, "The Lord is my Shepherd, I shall not want," the preacher paused, and then said "Not want what, David?" Without going into details this was the beginning of a very striking and dramatic dialogue between David and an imaginary questioner, and the rendering was such as to indicate that if our visitor had not chosen the Ministry, he could have been a first-rate actor.

After the service, everybody was discussing this wonderful dialogue and indeed the preacher made such a good impression that two or three years later he was invited again. When on this second occasion he announced his text as the Twenty-third Psalm we looked uneasily at one another, and when he continued with "Not want what, David?" we know that in the literal sense of the term we had indeed 'had it'.

Some seven or eight years later I was living in Nottingham. One day, in front of a large Methodist chapel, I saw an Anniversary placard announcing that on the following Sunday this same minister would be preaching. I decided to go. When he announced his text I feared the worst and any surviving hope was dashed when he began "Not want what, David?" Needless to say he rendered the dialogue entirely without notes, but if his memory had failed either for a word or a gesture, I could have prompted him. I wonder how many times he had given this highly original rendering of the Twenty-third Psalm?

Anniversary services are still held of course, but present day congregations are only a pale reflection of those we old folks remember. It is many a long year now since the stewards had to put seats in the aisles. The great traditions were broken, like so many others by the 1914-1918 war, and changes in the social structure make it seem less and less likely that there can be any turning back.

Our usual Sunday routine would seem formidable indeed to the present-day child. Sunday school, morning and afternoon, at Camden. Morning and evening service at St. Paul's though we didn't go in the evening until we were into our teens. There were alleviations. Sunday dinner was a high spot of the week, and we were free after three fifteen in the afternoon for quiet pursuits such as reading and country walks, both of which I enjoyed.

But I think the main reason we accepted it unquestioningly was that *everybody was doing it.* If we had been subjected to this routine while other boys were known to be swimming or playing cricket, we should have felt hard done by. As it was I didn't look upon Sunday as specially bright or specially dull. Just different.

As I mentioned earlier, Camden was a great social centre. There were weekday meetings of such organisations as the Wesley Guild, the Young Men's Club, the Boys' Brigade, and - a particularly strong feature this - the Band of Hope. To become a member one had to 'sign the pledge', the idea being to get hold of the children. There were frequent meetings at which the evils of drink were dwelt upon, and after an address by the chairman the children would give recitations and songs, all with a very strong 'blue ribbon' tendency. I recall one pretty little girl; dark hair, white dress - and red gloves. She was reciting a poem, each verse of which included the punch line 'and where there's drink there's danger' - and every time the line came round, out shot a red-gloved hand!

I still have in my possession a certificate for an essay I had written on 'Alcohol and Digestion' issued by the Lancashire and Cheshire Band of Hope Committee, and dated 1892. It is bordered in elaborate scrollwork in the Victorian style, and prominent in the foreground is an angel pouring out a cascade of liquid from a cask. I am not clear whether this is the 'water bright' we used to sing about or - in view of the cask - it is something alcoholic and undesirable she is disposing of!

There was plenty on the entertainment side. The Flower Queen, a simple little operetta though the word was never used, was produced many times with a guaranteed audience of mothers who had been press-ganged into making their daughters' costumes. Our inspiration was George's fiancée, Miss Temperley. She was quiet, with a soft voice, yet without needing to raise it she possessed the uncanny knack of organising a potentially unruly mob of youngsters, teaching the songs and putting the show on the road.

The girls were the flowers and the boys in the background formed a sort of chorus. The Flower Queen was of course the rose, and tact was sometimes needed to soothe ruffled feathers since there could only be one Queen. One year my sister Bessie had her turn, and I remember still how lovely she looked with her wreath of roses and masses of golden hair down to her waist.

Around Christmas and Whitsuntide there would be parties, where we played various games with Kiss in the Ring a perennial favourite, though in our Puritan assembly only a 'token' kiss consisting of a handshake was allowed. Sometimes Jack actually did kiss Jill, but should

*Bessie and Bertha (sitting) in the best frocks that young girls were wearing a hundred years ago.*

this happen a watchful superintendent always administered a rebuke calculated to prevent such a grave lapse becoming a precedent. Of course everybody knew everybody else, and I recall many a friendship between a young man and woman or even a boy and girl which, begun in church and Sunday school, ended in a happy marriage. This was my own fortunate experience.

If I seem to have said much more about nonconformists than about churchgoers, I must plead as my excuse that I was 'brought up chapel'. Let me atone to some extent by recounting a little story connected with the church. The sermon had been quite unusually long, and the children were becoming fidgety. Finally the parson exclaimed: "And what shall I say more?" and a little girl, one of the sufferers on the front row, answered promptly and clearly: "Pleath Thir, thay 'Amen'!"

At this point I will follow her advice.

# CHAPTER 8

# Home Life

There was really nothing unusual about 16, Leinster Gardens, either outside or in. It was a terrace house of a type still familiar today, with a narrow frontage and a long corridor by-passing the sitting rooms and leading to the kitchen. It was perhaps on a larger scale than the average. There was a back staircase intended for the use of a servant and also a large cool cellar, which provided us with an excellent substitute for a refrigerator. Altogether, and judged by working-class standards, it was a very good, commodious house.

There was a long garden at the front, and we defied convention by growing vegetables in it. At the back was just a yard where we kept pigeons and Nell, our old collie, had her kennel.

Leinster Gardens was quite a fashionable neighbourhood in the 'nineties, and it could be that we Littlers struck a rather plebeian note. We weren't rowdy, but there were a lot of us, and Number Sixteen was usually the scene of intense and varied activity, not all of it silent.

The pattern has changed much, even in my own lifetime. The best residential area is now in Higher Runcorn where in my boyhood, apart from a few grand houses, there were only muddy rutted lanes. Leinster Gardens bears the unmistakable air of having come down in the world, and the whole district is one of old property nearing the end of its useful span.

In saying there was nothing unusual about the house, I am judging it by the standards of seventy years ago. If a modern housewife were faced with the task of running it, especially in the absence of a maid tripping up and down those kitchen stairs, she could not be blamed for expressions of horror and alarm. It was made for work, everything in it and everything about it, and the situation was compounded by a forest of chimneys in Runcorn and Widnes belching forth black smoke. Grime and the reek of chemicals were all-pervading.

*Leinster Gardens*

Lace curtains had to be changed once a fortnight. No drip-dry; the soiled ones were washed and ironed - with flatirons heated on a gas ring.

The badly worn tiles on the kitchen floor could only be kept clean by scrubbing. It was an hour's work, and really needed to be done every day with a family the size of ours. 'Oilcloth' was the only alternative, and that would never have stood the wear.

The kitchen range was made of cast iron throughout, and was a precursor of the modern 'Aga'. It had three main parts. In the centre was an open fire which was lit each morning and fitted to swing over it was a hob on which the kettle stood. To the left of the fire was the oven, over which there was a shelf on which dough could be left to 'rise'. A boiler fitted with a tap provided the main supply of hot water, and this was installed to the right of the fire. We had no gas cooker and I doubt very much whether any such existed. We did have a gas ring which could also be used for boiling the kettle, but that was all. The range had a polished steel edge and, except for this edging which was cleaned with emery paper, the rest was blackleaded and polished once a week. It took two hours and much elbow-grease.

Cookery and diet were largely dictated by the characteristics of the range. It was ideal for baking bread, while Lancashire hotpot and rice pudding, both of which needed long slow cooking in an oven were 'staples' in most Victorian working class homes.

It has been said of the Scots that each new mouth was accommodated by the simple expedient of adding more water to the porridge, and the same principle applied to Lancashire hotpot. The ratio of mutton chops to potato steadily diminished as the size of the family increased.

Although we depended mainly on the oven for cooking, bacon and sausages were grilled with excellent results in a 'Dutch oven' which was placed on an iron stool in front of the fire, the fat dripping into a tray fitted into the bottom. The Sunday joint was roasted by hanging it from the hook of the 'jack', a clockwork contrivance which after being wound up turned with a 'click', so that the joint rotated to left and right; the origin no doubt of the phrase 'done to a turn'. The fat was collected in a tin below the joint, and used later to make the gravy. I have never elsewhere seen a 'jack' in action. I think father must have picked it up at a sale.

Probably the most serious lack in the Victorian diet was of fruit and fresh food. For the poor it was too expensive. For the better off it was bought and eaten for enjoyment, but with so little dietetic knowledge it wasn't thought of as essential to good health.

Lighting was by gas, but not what most people think of as 'gas' when they look back to the days immediately before the installation of electric current. All we had was the old-fashioned fish-tail burner. The light flickered, making reading and writing a terrible strain. I was glad when for a lengthy period father abolished it, and we had a paraffin lamp instead. It gave a very pleasant, steady light. The incandescent mantle came in somewhere about 1900 - at least as far as Runcorn was concerned. Outmoded now, it was a tremendous improvement on the old 'fish-tail'.

Household utensils made their own contribution to the general unhandiness. Stainless steel cutlery was still a thing of the future, so knives, forks and spoons were all of ordinary steel. It was one of my jobs to clean them on a Saturday morning so I can speak with knowledge. For the knives, I was provided with a board about twenty inches by four and covered with thin leather. Over this a block of brick dust was rubbed, and my teeth are set on edge even now as I write about it. The knife was rubbed on the board until it shone all over: a job rendered the more tedious by the knowledge that the knives would be just as bad again by next Saturday. The forks were cleaned with a moist rag that had previously been rubbed on 'Monkey Soap'. (The standard advertisement was 'Monkey Soap Won't Wash Clothes', the implication being I suppose that it would wash everything else). The cutlery, especially the knives, would be stained again in a day or so, but there simply wasn't the labour available to clean them oftener than once a week.

It must have been in or around the year 1890 that father returned from visiting an exhibition in Birmingham, and he was very excited about some kettles and saucepans he had seen. They were made of a metal that looked like silver but they were wonderfully light. He was describing aluminium, but at this time it was little more than a scientific curiosity. Our saucepans were nearly all of iron, black and sooty from boiling on the fire, and horrible to wash. One or two smaller ones were of brass.

But of all the defects in the 1890 house, those relating to plumbing and sanitation were the worst. Some of Runcorn's wealthier citizens may have been installing bathrooms by that time, but we hadn't one and neither had any of our neighbours.

Personal cleanliness wasn't really personal at all. It was part of a household manoeuvre, executed by long and hallowed tradition on a Friday night. We had a metal bath kept in a bedroom near the top of the back stairs. It was a laborious and not very safe proceeding. On bath night the boiler fire was lit and somebody had to carry supplies of hot and cold water upstairs, where there was no plumbing of any kind. However, I have no recollection of anything more serious occurring than a little horseplay with the cold water.

Sanitation was even more primitive than the plumbing, and here again our house would be typical. There was no indoor toilet, the privy being at the far end of the back yard. It stood over the front part of a brick lined pit, the back portion of which formed the 'midden'. The surrounding walls of privy and midden were continuous, and were roofed in. All household refuse was thrown into the midden by opening a door about two feet square, and the same door served to admit the 'night-soil' men when, at intervals of a few weeks, they emptied the pit.

This must have been one of the most unpleasant occupations that ever existed, and as the title indicates, it was a nocturnal one. Many a time I have wakened at dead of night to see the light from the torches flaring and flickering on the bedroom walls. Once awake I could hear the sound of shovelling, and the occasional stamp of a horse waiting in the street outside.

Although after each emptying the men sprinkled the floor of the pit with chloride of lime for disinfectant purposes, the general arrangement was highly insanitary. We had evidence of this in the great numbers of flies that invaded all houses at this period, but which disappeared when flush toilets became standard in Runcorn about the year 1905.

Spring cleaning was naturally a great feature, for not only did normal conditions of living give rise to a great deal of dirt, but Runcorn was only just across the Mersey from industrial Lancashire.

There may have been professional painters and decorators in Runcorn. There almost certainly were, but if so they were never employed at 16, Leinster Gardens. Father was at least half a century ahead of his time in the matter of DIY and every year he spearheaded the attack upon whichever part of the house was most in need of refurbishing. How I envied William, being allowed to paint the skirting boards! He was older of course, but he was also much more capable in practical matters. I never seemed to progress beyond the menial tasks of washing and scraping.

Father was a good workman, and sometimes his thoroughness was his undoing. More than once have I seen him give one turn too many to a screw, and split the wood. A commoner mishap was hitting his thumb with a hammer, in which case there was a strategic withdrawal on the part of the troops. Father wasn't really bad tempered but he was peppery, and we preferred to indulge our mirth at a safe distance. He usually relieved his feelings with an explosive: "Gosh beggar it!" - the nearest approach to strong language he ever permitted himself.

All my recollections are of painting. I don't recall any paper-hanging, and although some must have been done, it was probably very little. In parts of the house which were specially vulnerable, notably the hall and staircase and kitchen, Victorian wallpapers were there to last a lifetime. Almost, they were heirlooms. The fashionable colour was dark red, and they were varnished to increase their durability. They still survive here and there in the homes of elderly couples who have lived in the one place all their married lives.

There was nothing to correspond to distemper, much less emulsion. The nearest thing was lime wash, used for ceilings, back kitchens and outhouses.

From this brief description it will be clear that the house of 1890 was very deficient in labour saving devices. Add to that the washdays for ten and the baking days - for housewives like my mother would have held up their hands in horror at the idea of shop bread - and it becomes clear why it was held so desirable that a woman should be satisfied with her place in the home!

Inevitably the question is raised in one's mind: why had so little been done up to this time to lighten the labours of the housewife?

The obvious answer is that invention had not yet made any impact in this field. The practical applications of electricity were only in their infancy, and the domestic revolution which was to result within the next fifty years was beyond the range of even the prophets.

Another explanation was lack of incentive. The working classes provided a huge reservoir of cheap domestic labour, and this accounts also for the fact that the situation was made worse than it need have been by current fashions in furnishing. Rooms were overcrowded, and ornaments that were neither for use nor beauty were displayed by the score on pianos and mantelpieces and whatnots, while extra tables were imported for no other purpose than to hold still more. Our house was better than most in this respect, but father's sale going proclivities provided us with a steady flow.

We did not have much paid help, but in more prosperous working class homes such as ours the gap was filled in another way. The eldest daughter didn't normally go out to work. She helped at home, and even one willing pair of hands goes a long way towards making good the lack of modern conveniences.

In the year 1890 all the surviving children were living at home, and this with mother and father made ten of us. Let me first introduce you to my brother Samuel, always 'Sam' of course. He was now nineteen, and I mention him first, because when I was a baby and he was twelve, he found that quite without his own volition he had entered the nursing profession. It seems strange to us today that the mother of seventy years ago would have added to her never-ending labours by round-the-clock attendance on the latest baby, but so it was. Babies were never left if it was at all possible for somebody to be with them. In my case the problem was solved by the appointment of Sam as deputy.

A bit hard on a lad of twelve! To make matters worse, when I as the fourteenth child arrived, the pram which had served for I don't know how many preceding babies, had long since worn out. Anyway, when I was supposed to need an airing and he was available, poor Sam had to carry me, and this practice may have been the cause of my growing up with some slight physical irregularities.

When I was in my twenties an optician was fitting me with glasses; "I can't get it quite right," he said. "When your eyes are looking right through the centre of the lenses as they should, the lenses are not level with regard to the eyebrows. Were you by any chance dropped when you were a baby?" I said that having been made acquainted with my own early history, I thought this was very likely indeed.

Many years later, a dentist fitting me with some dentures was looking rather bothered. "Anything wrong?" I asked. "Well," he said, "you've got what we call a freak bite. That is, on one side your upper jaw projects over your lower, while on the other side it is the other way about. Do you happen to know whether you were dropped when you were a baby?" I explained that without having positive knowledge on the point, I had the very strongest suspicions.

About the same time I was having a new suit made at the tailor's, and the fit on the shoulders was not as good as it should have been. "I know what the reason is," he said. "You have one shoulder higher than the other. " I didn't give him a chance to speculate on the possible origin of this abnormality, and came up with my own explanation.

It should be mentioned here that a marked quality of my brother Sam as a grown man was his patience; and it may be that he acquired it during those formative years when the care of a baby brother was a first charge on his leisure time.

It was Sam who, when he was sixteen, decided that he wanted to be a sailor. In season and out of season he made it clear that a life on the ocean wave was the life for him. My parents did their best to put him off, but he was so insistent that they felt they had better take the matter seriously. On the other hand they really disliked the idea of his going to sea.

Mother thought she saw a possible solution to the problem. She had a brother, our Uncle Walter, who was a Hull trawler skipper, and in those days trawlers went out for a period of six weeks, after which they returned to their home port. Sam rejoiced greatly when she promised to write to uncle, asking if he could possibly be taken for a trial trip. Not for years afterwards did we learn that there was another part to her letter in which she said she would be only too pleased should he return completely cured of any desire for a seafaring life. In due course there was a reply. Uncle would be very pleased to take Sam for one of his six-week trips, but the lad must understand that there was no possibility of returning to port until the full time had expired. This was alright by Sam. If anything he thought six weeks a bit on the short side. So off he went.

It is a well known fact that the North Sea can be very rough. During this trip, and in Sam's opinion, it broke all records. For the first fortnight or so he was horribly sick, and often cold as well. He suggested to uncle that for once in a way the trawler might take him back to Hull and return to the fishing grounds, but this bright suggestion was promptly vetoed. He finished his six weeks, but never afterwards did he show the least desire to put to sea again.

Many years later, William expressed this same longing for the seafaring life and he also underwent the treatment, but on this occasion he was signed on as ship's cook, and spoke feelingly for years afterwards of the exquisite agony of cooking in a lurching galley for a crew of hungry sailors, and unable to keep even an egg-cupful of fluid down. Unlike Sam he never lost his love of the sea, but as a leisure activity and on his own terms.

Charles, or Charlie as we called him, was two years younger than Sam. He must have been about fifteen when the two went halves in a 'penny-farthing' bicycle. I don't suppose they paid much for it as it had had a number of previous owners, with a considerable drop in price at each exchange.

I was greatly interested in watching them learn to ride. Getting on was the great difficulty, and this it seemed could only be achieved by a long preliminary series of hops. However, they solved the problem at last and I often listened to them describing some wonderful ride they had had, longing for the time when I should be old enough to ride a 'penny farthing' myself.

They had a few accidents, always caused by the sudden cocking up of the back wheel accompanied by a corresponding downward movement of the rider! There was one period of about a fortnight when Sam's nose was badly bruised and of much more than normal size; but none of their accidents were really serious.

For some reason they frequently found it necessary to take the tyre off the front wheel. I was too young then to know what exactly was wrong, but looking back I think I can understand the trouble, my clue being that their repairs always called for the use of much cobbler's wax, or similar substance. The tyre must have been kept in position by the wax, but from time to time it would lift a little at one point, due perhaps to some extra jolt. After several such happenings it would be necessary to remove the tyre completely and fasten it down afresh.

During these proceedings there was of course a stage when some sixteen feet of tyre would be sprawling over the backyard. One morning after breakfast they had just reached this point when it was time to go to work, so operations had to be suspended. As I surveyed the field of recent activity, I was struck with a happy idea. Out of such a great length, it stood to reason that a little bit could well be spared, and getting a knife from somewhere I cut off a short length of seven or eight inches, and then subdivided it into about a dozen small pieces. I was able to go to school with a pocketful of 'india-rubbers'. Wealth indeed!

I had a profitable morning, trading my property for sweets, marbles and other oddments. After tea my brothers were at leisure to replace the tyre and I went out to watch them waxing down one little length after another. All went well until the final stage was reached. There was an unaccountable gap, and suddenly I realised that the piece I had cut off really mattered! I can still see Sam, his head bent as he looked carefully at the end of the tyre. "Charlie," he said, "somebody's been cutting this tyre. You can see the marks of the knife. " Charlie confirmed this diagnosis. A glance upwards and no doubt my red, uncomfortable face told the essential part of the story. I don't remember the sequel, and can only hope that they were able to procure a bit of old tyre somewhere and use it to fill up the gap.

Today, there is so much leisure amongst certain sections of the community that its use - or rather misuse - has joined the list of national problems. Books are written on the subject, in which well-meaning people put forward their ideas on how it should best be spent, schemes usually requiring the input of much public money. We had our problems in the 'nineties, but for youngsters this was not one of them. Leisure was a scarce commodity, even if Sam and Charlie hoarded enough of it to ride and repair a 'penny-farthing'.

On Saturday particularly, most people were busy 'getting ready for Sunday', when only essential work was done. Our house underwent a minor spring-clean, and this included certain operations in the backyard. The surface was partly tiled, partly cemented, and once a week it was swilled. Father would hold the hosepipe while William rubbed away at the spots indicated by the higher command. A visitor pausing there for a moment might easily have overheard a scrap of conversation. Yes - William suggesting that he and father should exchange broom and hosepipe for a few minutes, and the suggestion being promptly turned down. It would seem that the proper wielding of a hosepipe was a skill to be acquired only after long years of experience.

Even William rarely got the better of an argument with father. Once, when we both demurred at having to go out and shovel up manure to put round the rhubarb, father's references to 'stinking pride' were so withering that we were obliged to sally forth without further ado and run the gauntlet of jeering onlookers.

Fortunately, this was not one of the regular Saturday morning jobs. My knives were, and so were Sam's boots. They were all lined up outside the kitchen door: ten pairs of them; our Sunday best. Sam always got busy on them when he got in from his 'collecting round', which on a Saturday morning was only a short one. He used Berry's blacking. It was put on with a little water, then hard and long brushing was necessary to obtain a polish. Having tried both, I am of the opinion that cleaning a pair of shoes with 'Berry's' was at least twice the job it is today with a modern shoe polish.

It would have been possible of course for each of us to clean our own boots, but using Berry's blacking was such a messy business that by this method we had only one mess instead of ten.

My sister Nellie, after two hours spent in blackleading the kitchen range would be cleaning the downstairs windows. Those upstairs were done only once a fortnight and it entailed 'sitting out' on the sill with the window closed down so that it touched her knees. It looked and was a perilous business, and most homes now permit themselves the minor luxury of a window cleaner.

Nellie was then sixteen and deserved first place amongst hard workers. At half past four on a Saturday afternoon she would still be hard at it, scrubbing the kitchen floor. Young and strong, she made light of it, and had a great fondness for a practical joke.

I remember one, of which my eldest brother George was the victim. At about seven o'clock one evening he was hurrying to get changed for an appointment. There was a knock on the back door, and on opening it he could just make out, in the dark, the form of a bent old woman. It was hard to hear what she said, for she spoke in a low voice, but he caught something about 'hungry' and 'food', and dashed into the kitchen to find something. He soon returned, presenting the old woman with a slab of bread pudding which mother used to make up fairly often from the scraps, with additions to make them palatable.

He hurried back to complete his toilet, but two or three minutes later there was another knock, this time at the front door. He opened it, only to find another old woman enveloped in a shawl, with a racking cough that was pitiful to hear. Between bursts of coughing he caught something about 'hungry' and 'a few coppers'. "I don't approve of giving money at the door," he said, "but wait a minute," and he rush off down the passage. Really, this was most annoying - they must be telling each other - he snatched another piece of bread pudding and returned with it post haste. It was received with a peal of laughter, and in walked Nellie with two slabs of bread pudding. We all laughed too when we heard what had happened, but George said the interruptions would make him late for his appointment, and couldn't see anything funny in it at all, though he laughed about it later.

George was a very kind-hearted fellow as this incident shows, and generous to a fault. He and Sam were always full of wild cat schemes of one sort or another. Mostly they were George's, and Sam backed up as faithful henchman. In 1898 they decided to go on the Klondike Goldrush. This was no idle dream. Plans were advanced and they were assembling their kit, when father finally managed to put an end to the idea by persuading Miss Temperley, to 'name the day', and so the seal was set on another Camden romance.

This completes the introduction of all except my two small sisters, Bessie aged five and Bertha aged three, who were almost too young to count. You have met William as the lad who, some two years later, was to have the singular experience of being free from temptation for a whole week.

He had definite mechanical ability which occasionally led him into trouble. There was for instance the affair of the musical box. This was an instrument of which the essential part was a brass cylinder about nine inches by two, rather thickly and irregularly covered with short, thin brass spikes. There was a steel comb fixed parallel to the cylinder and almost touching it. After being wound up, the cylinder would turn, and as each brass spike caught against a tooth of the comb it gave out a rather sweet sound. The arrangement of the spikes was such that the instrument produced a tune. Actually, by altering the setting, it could be made to play four. The mechanism was mounted in a handsome mahogany box, and even in those days of cheap products it must originally have cost three or four pounds. Father had picked it up for a few shillings somewhere at a sale.

### George's Wedding in 1898 and the Fashions of the 'Nineties'

*George standing centre, the Bride is seated on his left. Mother (in a bonnet) stands behind him and to his left. Father is on her left, next to Sam's wife and Sam. Nellie is seated on the bride's right. Walter is kneeling (far left) with William standing behind him against the wall. Bessie and Bertha are on the front row, holding their lace hats.*

Of the four tunes 'Home, Sweet Home' is the only one I now recall. The rendering was sweet but dismally slow. It needed to be three or four times as fast. Because of this we had long since ceased to use the instrument. One day William came to me with the air of one having an important communication to make. "You remember how horribly slowly that musical box plays its tunes?" he said. Yes I remembered very well. "Just come and listen to it now!" he said.

We went to the instrument. "First listen to it before I do anything to it," - he started it off on 'Home, Sweet Home' which it played at its usual funereal pace. "Now listen," he said, as he pushed a small wooden wedge under some part of the mechanism. I agreed that there was a great improvement, though the rendering was still a little on the slow side. "No trouble at all," was the reply, "I simply push the wedge a little further, like this." Sure enough, the tempo might now be described as Allegro, if anything a bit on the fast side.

"You see there's no limit to it laddie," he said, and he made one or two more adjustments to the wedge. The musical box was now giving the fastest rendering of 'Home, Sweet Home' I had ever heard in my life. It was fairly whizzing along.

"No limit," he said excitedly, "simply no limit!" He gave one more push to the wedge, and - zr-zr-zr-zr; the cylinder turned backwards at a furious pace, and dozens of those little brass spikes flew off in every direction. Our musical box was finished. It couldn't even be wound up!

Some seconds of horrified silence supervened, and then he gasped out "What will father say?"

We never knew the answer to that one. The writer of Ecclesiastes says "There is a time to keep silence and a time to speak," and although we were not secretive youngsters we agreed that this was a time for keeping silence, at least until such time as father should start making enquiries. Fortunately he never did and the crime went undiscovered.

Father's penchant for sale going has been mentioned several times. He was a great man for sales, and the contrivance which was William's undoing was not his only flutter in the musical instrument field. He once got so carried away by the bidding that he found himself in possession of a pipe organ, but as there was no possibility of ever getting it in through the front door, it had to be sold again without our even having seen it. It was a great disappointment to we children, who felt it would have made a most impressive addition to the Leinster Gardens parlour.

If I have given the impression that life held nothing else but work, this was far from being the truth. We played with enthusiasm all the usual outdoor games which differed little from those of the present day, but admittedly indoor recreation was much more limited. There was of course no radio or television, but we could and did play draughts, tiddly-winks and one or two card games, 'Snap' and 'Happy Families' being the chief favourites. While we were so engaged, mother would be busy with her sewing or darning needle, while father would be reading the Liverpool Echo which in those days cost a halfpenny. Often after he had been reading it for an hour or so, apparently with the greatest interest, I have seen him toss it on one side with a gesture of disgust and the remark: "I don't know why I go on taking t'blessed paper. There's nowt in it!"

As far as games on Sunday were concerned, the practice varied. In my own home, quiet card and board games were allowed, but in others they were strictly forbidden. In still others a middle line was adopted, and in one home with which I was very well acquainted 'Ludo' was allowed, providing the opposing sides labelled themselves 'Israelites', 'Philistines' and so forth. It was a kind of harmless bargaining with the Almighty.

On Sunday evenings we seemed to turn more naturally to reading than to games, and this was often our preference on other evenings too. We had a fair supply of books, including many bound volumes of the 'Chatterbox' and the 'Boy's Own Paper', and a further great resource was the Free Library where one could be led unerringly to the best books by the concentration of aroma that clung to them.

There was no outstanding musical talent in the family but one or two of us could play a little on the piano, while Sam could play the cornet, George the clarinet and Charlie the viola. Father too, with his concertina, could produce a tune which, though not quite up to recital standards, was at any rate recognisable.

Mustering some or all of these resources and with the rest of us singing, we passed many a pleasant hour on Sunday evenings with our favourite hymns, and if our performance was somewhat lacking in refinement, I am sure it would have obtained full marks for vigour.

Though it may seem strange that, in a home with such a strong religious background, we didn't go to Chapel on Christmas day, it is the case that by 1890 the Dickensian Christmas was well established, and it was entirely associated in my mind with secular joys. *

The gifts reflected the standard of living at that time. A sock contained the traditional apple and orange, a handful of nuts, a twist of sweets, and perhaps a novelty like a toffee mouse, still popular today. In addition there were one or two stocking-size toys and a 'Big Present' which might be a penknife or a doll, or for the younger children a box of bricks or a skipping rope. The great prize was the annual edition of the 'Chatterbox' which, though given to a different child each year, was regarded as public property and read by all. The recipient simply had pride of ownership!

Being such a large family we made our own fun, and I don't recall it being diminished in any way through being conducted on strictly teetotal principles. The religious aspect of the day was recognised in the evening when, with sufficient numbers to muster soloists and chorus, we sang well-known and much loved excerpts from Handel's 'Messiah'.

The great communal event was the Camden Christmas Party at which we met up with our friends, high spirits being checked but briefly by the need for 'grace'. Teachers and helpers, as well as mothers and fathers, toiled and contributed willingly to give us the time of our lives.

* Attendance at a Christmas Day service was probably a more common practice amongst Church goers, Holy Communion being central to Church of England worship. This did not apply to the same extent amongst non-conformists. Always known as The Sacrament of the Lord's Supper, it was usually held once a month after an evening service, but many regular worshippers didn't stay for it.

Though the author doesn't mention it, the exception to this may have been the Celebration which always took place on the first Sunday afternoon of the new year, and must certainly have been rooted in long tradition. I well remember that my maternal grandparents took me to this on one occasion in the early 'twenties, when I was a small child. There was a large congregation, and the use of individual communion cups slowed the proceedings down to a point where I thought they would never end.                    *M. S.*

# CHAPTER 9

# Farnworth

When I revisited Farnworth recently after a lapse of many years, I would not have recognised it but for one or two focal points such as the Parish Church. It is now just a suburb of Widnes, and the good farm land which once surrounded the village has been parcelled out into gardens for neat rows of semi-detached villas.

But the immediate vicinity of Aunt Margaret's cottage has escaped, as though by a miracle, from the steady encroachment of a growing industrial town. It is only about a mile and half from Farnworth, but Hunt's farm is still hard by, and the pits where we used to fish as children.

The cottage itself vanished long ago. It was old and decayed as I knew it, and could never have survived until now. The plaster was mouldering on the damp walls, and the floorboards and narrow stairway were rickety with dry rot. Its physical disappearance matters little, so strongly does it live on in memory, just as it always was.

It stood about three miles in a northerly direction from the Widnes end of the Old Bridge (the same railway bridge on which my father worked, it came to be called the Old Bridge to distinguish it from the Transporter Bridge, opened in 1905 and soon to be replaced by a new road bridge). It is a simple matter now to reach the spot because a corporation bus service does the journey in about a quarter of an hour, dropping one off at the 'Black Horse', a modern hotel built long since the days when Aunt Margaret was alive. The cottage was about five minutes' walk down Cronton Lane, a sharp turn to the left at the meeting point of roads just by the 'Black Horse'.

On fine Saturdays mother would often provide William and myself with a packed lunch and twopence for crossing the Old Bridge. A footpath ran beside the track, protected from it by high criss-crossed girders, and an old man in a shelter like a sentry box collected a toll of one penny for the return journey at the Runcorn end.

**The Railway Bridge**

An early photograph taken from the Widnes side of the river.

H.F. Starkey

This was our route to Farnworth as we called it, though Aunt's cottage was quite some distance away. There was no bus in those days, and the journey from door to door would be about four miles. We had to walk through Widnes but the mean streets and smoking chimneys were soon behind us and we were out in open country.

Quick and easy access to the country was one of our childhood's greatest compensations when there were no cars, no public transport other than the railways, and no long holidays. The annual fortnight in August was an unheard-of thing for working-class people and holidays - even honeymoons - were usually only a day. But with the population little more than half of what it is today, and the necessity for men to live near their place of work, there wasn't the pressure on open space. We did have the countryside on our doorstep. It was part of our lives and with us all the time, not something to be attained with much planning and preparation on a set occasion.

The real attraction at Farnworth was the fishing. The rods were two-piece bamboo affairs which cost sixpence each. The lines were a penny, and hooks were to be had at four for a halfpenny from Dutton's in Devonshire Square. We liked to keep a supply of these as losses were fairly frequent.

When we reached the smithy, which stood on the site of the present 'Black Horse', there was always an unpleasant encounter to be negotiated. The blacksmith's apprentice was in the habit of calling out very insulting remarks such as " 'ello, gooin' fishin' are ye? Baitin' wi' saucers and catchin' ponmugs more like it, ah reckon!" So when we were passing we tried to conceal the tell-tale rods by carrying them close to our bodies, but not always with success.

I must give some account of Aunt Margaret because for three years or more, from the time that I was six and he was nine, William and I were frequent visitors to her cottage.

She was not really our aunt, but father's cousin. She lived by herself and was very poor. She was very good-looking, with a clear skin, bright brown eyes and a pleasant expression. Tall and spare, she was even then, when only in her early fifties, slightly bent from heavy toil in the fields. Whenever work was available, she worked for a shilling a day on Ellison's farm, but in bad weather even this tiny source of income dried up. She was probably in receipt of Parish relief, for although she grew her own potatoes I don't see how else she could have managed to live. On Sunday mornings she rarely missed going to church, from which she would bring back two small loaves, presumably an allowance from some charitable bequest.

William and I once asked mother whether she had ever been married? This produced an odd reaction. We were told that it was no business of ours, and we were warned that when talking to Aunt Margaret we were to keep well away from the subject, which we did. I have a very vague recollection of hearing at some time that she had been married, but discovered after a few weeks that her husband had a wife still living. On making this discovery she had left him.

Otherwise I know nothing of her early life; whether she had been born in or around Farnworth or whether, as her isolation would suggest, she had - unusually for a country girl in those days - travelled the twenty miles from her native Ince and crossed the Mersey to be married.

Years after her death I visited Farnworth churchyard, and with the help of the sexton found her grave. The stone bears the inscription:

In affectionate memory of Samuel Copeland,
who departed this life April 19th 1882, aged 42.
Also of Margaret Farrel,
died Feb. 10th 1913, aged 72.

A probable guess is that Samuel Copeland was the bigamous husband, and that although she would not live with him, her love had outlasted the long years of separation and she had wished to be buried in the same grave.

During the school holidays we often made quite lengthy visits to Aunt Margaret; on one occasion we stayed as long as three weeks. This meant taking a change of clothes, and as well as this we were always given a small packet, with instructions to take great care of it and hand it over as soon as we arrived. No doubt it contained money.

Two small boys on their own would naturally run into trouble now and again. I have a vivid recollection of a certain occasion at Hunt's farm. This was not much more than a stone's throw from Aunt's cottage, and as the Hunts were very friendly people we often found ourselves over there.

In the yard was a cesspool which provided drainage for the stables and shippons, and on this pool there floated part of a plank about a yard long and nearly a foot wide. It seemed to me to have great possibilities as a boat, and I could see myself making joyous cruises up and down the pool. This was admittedly rather smelly, but one cannot have everything. I mentioned my idea to William. After looking critically first at the wood and then at me, he said he thought it might 'bear' me all right, but would not be safe for him because he was so much heavier.

I tried to embark, but no sooner had I stepped on to the plank then it upended, and I found myself in the cesspool. This would not be more than a foot deep, but unfortunately I had fallen not on my feet, but almost horizontally. I was back on terra firma within a few seconds, but never in my life before had I been in such a disgusting condition. It must be said in fairness that William did his best. He made a preliminary effort by scraping me with a pocket knife, at the same time keeping his nose pinched with his left hand - an unnecessarily offensive gesture, I thought.

Unfortunately there was no pump handy, or the procedure would have been obvious. As it was, the best we could do was to have recourse to a nearby ditch, but it soon became plain that there was no hope of 'getting by' as far as Aunt Margaret was concerned. We had to go back to the cottage and await her return from the day's work of hoeing turnips, and this was not until half past five. I was then able to change into my Sunday suit while she washed the dirty one, not without such observations as: "Maybe boys will be boys, but that don't count sailing on a stinking old cesspool," and much more to the same effect.

The Hunts, upon whose farm this unfortunate incident took place, had three sons. The youngest one, Sam, was about William's age and we spent a lot of time with him. He was able to give us useful hints about fishing, and he also showed us how to make a wonderful bird trap out of four bricks and a few twigs. We never did much trapping ourselves, but we watched his efforts and often saw him catch starlings, or 'shepsters' as they are called in Cheshire. He was well-versed in country lore and taught us amongst other things how to recognise the call of different birds. A specially characteristic one was the corncrake, or landrail. It was common then, but one rarely hears it now.

Mr Hunt had a brother Tom who lived in a sort of gypsy caravan not many yards from the house. Though Tom had periods of sobriety often lasting for weeks, he was apt from time to time to go on what would now be termed a 'bender' when he would be drunk for days together. My impression was that Mrs Hunt had flatly refused to have him living in the house, while her husband out of brotherly loyalty didn't like to turn him away, so that the caravan represented a compromise between their two points of view.

This caravan greatly intrigued us, never having seen anything like it before. We would look for excuses to go in, and always received a warm welcome from old Tom. The odd thing is that he never tired of addressing us on the evils of drink, exhorting us constantly never to take the first glass. No 'Sons of Temperance' orator could have put the case more effectively, and he seemed to be perfectly sincere. No doubt he saw quite clearly how drink had been the ruin of his own life, and it was out of genuine, kindly concern for us that he spoke as he did.

The Hunt family disappeared from the farm many years ago, and the old farmhouse has given place to a more modern building. Some of the outbuildings are much as I remember them, but a certain cesspool of odoriferous memory has been filled up. A strange thing is that nearly seventy years ago, on the gable end of the barn facing the road, was a pear tree which cropped very late in the year, yielding what the Hunts called 'winter pears'. There is still pear tree in that position, and the present occupants of the farm tell me that it is a late cropper. Surely a pear tree would not continue fruiting for all those years? Perhaps the present tree is a lineal descendant of the one we knew. Or, who knows? There is the old saying about 'pears for your heirs'!

Aunt Margaret worked at Ellison's farm, a good half mile from Hunt's and in the opposite direction. At Ellison's there were two pits where you could catch perch. Here we used earthworms for bait, and the perch would bite really savagely. We had some very lively times at those pits.

But my most abiding recollection of Ellison's farm is associated, not with perch but with cows. Many a time at about four in the afternoon I watched them winding their leisurely way to the farmyard and thence to the cowshed or 'shippon'. I liked, too, to watch them being milked. One afternoon I asked a farm-hand who was milking to let me take his place, but not unnaturally, he refused. If I wanted to milk a cow, he said, I should have to ask Mr Ellison's permission.

Accordingly, I sought him out. "If you please Mr Ellison," I said in my politest tones, "would you let me milk a cow?"

"What?" he said. He was rather deaf so I repeated my request, this time more loudly.

"Milk a cow?" he laughed immoderately. "Milk a cow, well, that's a good 'un! No, my lad, tha' can't milk a cow. T'owd cow 'ud 'ave a fit if *tha* milked it," and he ambled off, still chuckling to himself at the very idea.

Clearly there was nothing more to be done for the moment, and I returned to think over the situation. At first the idea of milking a cow had been nothing more than a passing whim, but it had now developed into an obsession. There was nothing in the world I so much desired as to milk a cow. Besides, it was obviously so easy. You just grasped one of those curious projections they called 'teats' and then moved your hands up and down. I brooded over the subject until bedtime and then 'slept on it' as the saying goes. In the morning the solution had come to me, one so simple that I wondered that I had never thought of it before.

That afternoon I reached the farmyard about a quarter of an hour before the cows might be expected, and went right to the far end of the shippon. There was a gangway up the middle, a yard or more wide, with stalls to right and left for the individual cows, these stalls being at right angles to the gangway. There were perhaps ten of them on each side. I placed myself with pail and milking-stool and waited for my cow.

In due course she arrived. I gave two or three tugs in what seemed to be the approved fashion, and then everything began to go wrong. For some reason not then clear to me, there was no satisfying, rhythmic spurt of milk into the pail, and the cow appeared to take fright. She backed and turned round, and with much difficulty because of the incoming line of other cows, made her way down the gangway.

There was great confusion, and it was a few minutes before I was able to make my exit. No sooner had I regained the farmyard then I had the ill-luck to encounter Mr Ellison. I cannot say how he knew that I was the cause of all the trouble, but he certainly did, and for the next two or three minutes he seemed to be in imminent danger of apoplexy. I must count myself lucky to have escaped a sound thrashing. Two or three days later he told my Aunt that this particular cow had 'gone dry'. That brief and unexpected encounter with a small boy intent upon milking her had evidently upset her nervous system. I never made any further attempt, and to this day there is a definite gap in my education - I cannot milk a cow.

It did not occur to me until years afterwards that this escapade had placed me in real danger. A frightened cow is a dangerous animal, and instead of retreating from the stall as she did, she might easily have gored me, and from that confined space I should have stood little chance of escape.

An adventure of William's on the same holiday might equally well have ended in disaster. About half a mile from Aunt's cottage was Pex Hill, a rough area of broken sandstone covered with bracken. It was full of little irregularities, and in the side of one of the slopes was a hole just about large enough to admit a man on hands and knees. To Sam Hunt and the local residents it was known as Peggy's Cave, and they were all rather afraid of it. If you went through that hole, they said, you could wriggle along for a few minutes, and then you came to a point where it opened out into a sort of room, big enough to stand up in. In that room was something dreadful: a skeleton sitting up in an old chair, as far as I remember. They admitted however that this was only local hearsay, not knowing anybody who had been in to see.

"Why not go in and find out for certain?" William asked.

They replied quite frankly that they wouldn't dare.

"Nobody would dare," they added. "You wouldn't!"

If there was one thing William could never resist, it was a dare. "Oh! wouldn't I?" he answered.

He took off his coat, wriggled through the hole on his hands and knees and was soon lost to sight. We waited, and about ten minutes later he reappeared facing us as he emerged from the hole, so we knew that at some point in his journey he must have been able to turn round. We were of course all agog to hear about that skeleton! He told us that, going forward on his knees, he hadn't found much trouble in getting along. After about five minutes he had come to an enlargement, big enough to stand up in, but nothing like the size of a room. It contained neither chair nor skeleton. He had then returned.

He had emerged safely, but the disturbance he caused in wriggling his way forward might easily have brought about a fall of sand and stones which would have blocked his exit.

These two incidents underline a problem which sooner or later presents itself to all conscientious parents. They wish their children to develop initiative and resource, but this is only possible if they are given a good deal of freedom and independence.

Insistence on obedience had always been a strong feature of our upbringing, and it was partly aimed at ensuring our physical safety. They hoped that it would provide for likely eventualities during our visits to Farnworth, and it was impressed upon us that we were to obey to the letter any instructions we were given. The risk lay in the fact that we were very young, that Aunt Margaret was a very busy and overworked person, and in the absence of any ruling we used our own judgement when a choice of action presented itself. Nobody could anticipate that I might want to milk a cow, or that William might wish to know whether there was any truth in that skeleton story.

Returning to our life at Farnworth; my cesspool misadventure and the untoward occurrence at Ellison's farm stand out with special clearness, but there were plenty of other minor incidents, and I can see looking back that we must often have irritated and sometimes really worried our long-suffering Aunt. It is no wonder then that we often heard such expressions as "Now just you wait until I see your mother, and as sure as you're alive I'll tell her what naughty boys you've been!" We were not unduly disturbed by these remarks, banking as we did on the fact that a visit from mother was most unlikely.

Then one morning a letter arrived with the news that she proposed coming that very day!

In emphasising that mother relied very much on 'moral 'suasion' as the best means of correcting wrong-doing, I may have given the impression that we had little to fear in the way of condign punishment. That is very far from the truth. Though she had not much use for the stick, she could and did punish in other ways, sometimes very severely. We knew for example that in the present instance she was quite capable of saying, "It is clear from what your Aunt has said that you cannot be trusted to behave properly when you are on your own, so this will be the last of your Farnworth visits. You will be going back with me tonight!" It would have hurt her terribly to give such a decision, but having done so nothing would have made her alter it. With past experience to guide us we would not even have made the attempt.

And so the arrival of the letter plunged us into the deepest gloom. It is said that when a man is drowning he has a rapid vision of all his past life. That may or may not be true, but certainly during the hours that followed the receipt of mother's letter all our holiday misdoings paraded themselves before us, and as we recalled them to each other, our gloom deepened.

Mother arrived about six o'clock and soon we were all seated at tea, a most worrying meal for William and me. At last came the fateful question: "Well Margaret, and have the boys been good?"

So far as we were concerned, you could have heard a pin drop. And then - were we awake or dreaming? - came the answer; "Well Sarah, you know what boys are. They get a bit lively now and again, but that's nothing. Take 'em altogether and you couldn't have two better lads. Always very willing to do anything they can to help, and if I've told them to do this, or not to do that, they've always been very obedient. They're a credit to you, Sarah."

We almost lost our balance, but recovered it immediately in case mother's suspicions should be aroused. We were all gratitude, but quite at a loss to understand this change of front. It was agreed between us in secret conclave that there was no accounting for the ways of grown-ups, and there we had to leave the matter.

The escapades which had almost led to our downfall were only incidental. Fishing was our main holiday occupation. As well as the pits at Ellison's farm where we caught the perch, there was one not a stone's throw from Aunt's cottage where jacksharp abounded. For these, we simply tied a worm on the end of a rush and the sport was fast and furious. We could catch a dozen in next to no time. Sometimes we would get two at once, one on each end of the worm.

But we didn't often fish for jacksharp. We looked upon it as rather a kid's game whereas we were, well, not exactly grown up, but certainly not what you could call 'kids'. Our main quarry was roach. (We called them 'dace', but I know now that they were really roach), and our usual fishing ground was Hunt's pits. Starting from near the farm, we skirted a rather long field hedge, and in a depression at the end were the two pits.

If as a result of fishing for two hours we came away with two or three small roach, we were well satisfied. We kept them alive in a toy bucket of water, taking them home at the end of the holiday, and some of them lived for months. On two occasions we landed a real whopper - to use our own term - so big that we asked Mrs Hunt to let us weigh it on a pair of household scales she possessed. In each case the weight was two ounces, and our cup of joy was full.

Truth compels me to add that my own catches were very few and far between, and William must have caught at least three times as many as I did. I know now where my technique was at fault, albeit too late in the day to be of any help. At the same time I did have one great piece of luck, for I caught the second of the two ounce 'whoppers'. I can still recall something of the ecstasy with which I saw it jumping about on the grass just after I had landed it. On one occasion, many years afterwards, I caught a fish weighing nine pounds, but I felt nothing like the rapture that accompanied the catching of the two ounce roach.

We associated with some rough types at those pits, but though they were mostly lads in their 'teens and twice our size, they never did us any harm. Bad language we were used to and took no notice of it. What did hold us in thrall were the stories they told of the mighty fish they had caught, and those still mightier that had got away. It never occurred to us to doubt their veracity, though the chance of a 'pig fish' which weighed a hundredweight inhabiting one of Hunt's pits, was decidedly more remote than that of a monster inhabiting Loch Ness!

The only fish we ever saw them catch bore a striking resemblance to the ones we caught ourselves, and many a time have I seen them slit these open with a knife, gut them after a fashion and eat them raw.

There was one other fishing ground, a rather mysterious one. Just opposite 'The Black Horse' was a tree-covered area which used to be called the Plantation. It was separated from the road by a wall said to be built of 'pressed brick' and to have cost a thousand pounds. A thousand pounds! It was a mind-boggling sum! Maybe it had though, because it was one of the longest walls I ever saw. At the end near 'The Black Horse' was a lodge, and near the other end, and inside the wall of course, was a very large house.

In our day the lodge was lived in by some very friendly people called Platt. No doubt they had instructions not to let anybody into the grounds, but when the people at the big house were away they would sometimes invite us to fish in 'The Lake', a large pond really, though not very deep. To us there was always something a bit eerie about this particular fishing ground. For one thing we had promised to be as quiet as possible, because the Platts were afraid if we were heard by people outside, a report might ultimately reach their employers. So we spoke only in low tones, glancing apprehensively now and again amongst the trees - you never knew who or what might be lurking in the undergrowth!

Even the roach we caught in the lake were unusual, for they were of a very pale golden colour. Much later we realised that they were not roach at all, but small carp. By our humble standards, the sport here was very good, no doubt because the pond was fished so little.

I revisited the Plantation a little while ago, and was rather sorry to find that there is no longer any air of mystery about it. Part of that wonderful thousand-pound wall has been removed and a section of the grounds is open to the public. One is now free to walk all round the lake, and it no longer has the sinister appearance of bygone days because some of the surrounding trees have been felled. Whether one could still fish there successfully for small carp I don't know. There is nothing to indicate that public access includes fishing rights!

As our largest catch was only two ounces, it is plain that our fishing activities could not go far towards supplementing the diet at Aunt Margaret's. Our main interest was not in eating them but in keeping them alive, and using a toy bucket as a temporary home we transferred them to more roomy quarters when we got back to Runcorn. Here there was a circular bath about a yard across and perhaps a foot deep, and we were very pleased when father said we might use it. We put it in the back yard, filled it with water, and in it we put our seven precious fish. The arrangement seemed perfect.

All went well for two or three days, and then one morning when we counted the fish there were only six. The morning after there were only five! This provided a sinister parallel to the story of the 'Ten Little Nigger Boys', and when we recalled that last tragic line "And then there were none," we decided that something must be done about it.

We suspected a cat, Ginger, which belonged to our neighbour Mrs Beckett, but suspicion is not proof. Fortunately that morning, while our fish still numbered five, we obtained the evidence we needed. We saw Ginger lurking near our fish bath, quite obviously loitering with intent to commit a felony. We chased him off, but several times during that day we had to repeat the process. Clearly, Ginger was a first-class menace. We talked it over and decided that Ginger must be shot. A blood-thirsty decision perhaps, but we were feeling very sore over the loss of our fish, and worried about the threat to the others.

We had no air-gun, but we did have bows and arrows which we were always making ourselves, and to the end of each arrow we bound a sharp nail. Then we lay in ambush in the coal-shed. We waited there for two hours but no Ginger appeared and the plan had to be abandoned. We brought the fish indoors as a temporary measure and a few days later mother rejoiced our hearts by buying us a gold-fish bowl, in which we managed to keep them alive for several months.

I have often wondered what would have happened if Ginger had appeared. We should almost certainly have hit him for the distance was less then five yards, but in view of the proverbial 'nine lives' and his thick fur, I doubt if we should have killed him. He would have returned to Mrs Beckett in a panic stricken state, a highly mobile pin cushion with two arrows sticking in his fur. Uncanny instinct would have brought Mrs Beckett to our front door, pressing for exemplary punishment to be meted out to the would-be assassins. All things considered, it was providential that the affair ended as it did.

It was on one of our later visits to Farnworth, when I was eight and a half, that I put into execution a long-cherished plan. This had been maturing for some time, receiving fresh impetus whenever we went with Aunt Margaret to church on a Sunday morning.

Coroner's Lane which led to the village of Farnworth, branched off from the main road just by the Plantation Lodge. This was the way we always went, and at each end of the lane was a most exciting signpost which said: 'To Warrington'.

I had heard that at Warrington the River Mersey was so narrow that it was crossed by a small bridge, and that it was possible to reach Runcorn by walking the six or seven miles from Farnworth to Warrington, and then on the other side of the Mersey, walking another six or seven miles from Warrington to Runcorn. It would be a great achievement, I thought, to do the complete journey.

I can give no logical reason as to why I should have wanted to do this. Perhaps it was the same spirit moving me as would move George to make his plans to go on the Klondike Goldrush, or William who years later made a determined but unsuccessful attempt to join the Canadian North West Mounted Police, a calling which would have suited him perfectly.

I had more than a suspicion that my plan would receive the blessing of neither my Aunt nor William, so I said nothing about it. I managed to give both of them the slip, and set forth one fine Saturday morning. It was the eighth of August 1891, and I know the date so exactly for a reason that will presently appear.

I had no difficulty in finding my way to Warrington, for signpost after signpost gave me the necessary direction. Fortunately the roads were perfectly safe, because this was long before the days of motor cars. I remember very little of the journey except that at intervals of a mile or so there were slabs of concrete labelled 'Traveller's Rest' and carrying the information that they were supplied by Sir Gilbert Greenall, who was, I believe, a brewer. I didn't rest at any of them. I wanted to reach Warrington and so complete the first stage of my odyssey. Never once - so thoughtless can a child be - did I reflect that my disappearance would be the cause of acute anxiety to Aunt Margaret, to say nothing of William.

I reached Warrington in safety, but at this point my plans began to go awry. They had taken no account of the fact that I should have to cross the town, and this forgotten item was my undoing.

I was tired and hungry. Because it was unfamiliar, the town seemed huge and terrifying. I knew I must find the bridge across the river but I had no idea which way to go, and I was afraid if I started enquiring I might be asked a lot of questions.

I would like to be able to say that in spite of all these difficulties I finally reached Runcorn, but it just would not be true. I wondered aimlessly around the town and then sat down on a doorstep and dissolved into tears.

A boy of fifteen or so carrying a butcher's basket asked me what the trouble was, and I told him.

"So you've come from Farnworth?"

"Yes," I said.

"Then you'd better go back there. Your Aunt will be wondering what has happened to you. Come along with me," he said.

I accompanied him to the station and he bought me a half-fare ticket, price threepence, to Farnworth. Before long a train came in and I soon reached Farnworth station. I didn't know I had to give up my ticket and nobody asked me for it. It came into mother's possession and she kept it for many years, so that is why I know so exactly the date of my great adventure.

A final walk of over half a mile brought me home. Both Aunt Margaret and William had been very worried. Aunt indeed had been almost frantic thinking that perhaps I had fallen into one of the pits where we so often fished, and been drowned. If the episode did nothing else, it taught me that one should spare a thought sometimes for the other person's point of view.

I have often thought of the lad with the butcher's basket. Probably threepence was a full quarter of his day's earnings.

"How far that little candle throws his beams!
So shines a good deed in a naughty world."

# CHAPTER 10

# Amusements and Recreations

The past is recreated in the mind's eye, and when I think of the outdoor games that boys used to play when I was at school, the mental image is always one of a patch of waste ground with a group of lads kicking a ball about on it. The ball is some kind of substitute for a football, and the goal posts are represented by untidy heaps of clothing.

The picture is significant in two ways. Because there were fewer counter attractions, boys played outdoor games much more than they do now. There was no radio or television to keep them inside, and there were none but primitive means of mechanical locomotion. A present-day teenager is more likely to be tinkering with an old motor bike, or - if he is a keep fit enthusiast - he may be out every fine weekend, covering long distances with the local cycling club.

The other significant point is the patch of waste ground. When the need was never greater, the provision of playgrounds and playing fields for children and young people was hopelessly inadequate. The changes in the Leinster Gardens district may well be typical in this respect. There were three such waste patches in my boyhood, all well patronised. Two have now been taken over for building, but the 'Big Pool' opposite our house has been filled in and laid out as a recreation ground. It served as a reservoir for the locks on the Bridgewater canal, but with abandonment of sections of the canal, it became redundant. (Its secondary function of providing a first class breeding ground for mosquitoes in summer, has also come to an end).

One playground was available to us just as it is now, and that was the school yard. From personal observation there seems to be little variation in traditional games. Certainly there has been no decline in the popularity of 'hit' and 'hide and seek' amongst small children. They 'count out', as we used to do, with various little rhymes and jingles, but I should like to know whether in Cheshire they still shout "Balla me not on," or "Balla me first turn. " This was a substitute for 'counting out'. In hide and seek for instance, the last to be in with his 'balla' had to be the seeker. It always struck me as a most curious phrase, but years later its probable derivation occurred to me. It could well be a corruption of "By your leave me," so that "By your leave, me not on," became "Balla me not on. "

During the quarter hour break in the school yard, a favourite game was 'fighting on horseback'. One boy, preferably of sturdy build, would be the horse with a lighter boy as rider, and two such pairs would do battle. The horse had the job of keeping his feet, which was by no means easy, while each rider tried to pull the other from his mount. Torn and dirty collars were the usual outcome, and sometimes a boy would be injured by a fall on the cobbled ground. After two or three days Gaffer Jordan would become aware of what we were doing and jousting would be banned. Within a few months however the prohibition would be forgotten, and the game would once more enjoy a short run.

If William and I were late home from school, it was usually because we had beguiled the tedium of the way with 'Bob along'. This was a simple game played at the edge of the road, and it started off by each of us selecting a stone - easy enough in those days of Macadam surfaces. I would put my stone down, whereupon William aimed at it from a point about two yards behind, and if he scored a hit he was 'one up'. It would often be that his stone would rebound on mine and still be behind it. In that case he was entitled to a second shot, and this continued until his stone was in front of mine. It was then my turn. Homeward progress was of necessity slow under such circumstances and we rarely continued it for more than about fifty yards.

Another great game was marbles, which could be played in any side street. Although marbles were for sale in the shops, I never met with a boy who had bought them. There seemed to be a large floating stock in existence. Some boys would have two or three hundred, others as few as a dozen, but all had some.

I imagine that few boys of today would know how to play marbles in accordance with the traditional rules. These are very complicated, and there is plenty of room for skill. A good player would often find his stock mounting at the rate of two or three dozen a day.

Often when a group of boys was playing, a much bigger boy would rush to the ring and steal the marbles. Such cads were known as 'crumpers'. Occasionally a few small boys would successfully combine against a crumper and there would be a most satisfying wiping off of old scores.

In many parts of Cheshire, and very likely elsewhere, there is - or was - a curious tradition of playing marbles on Good Friday. In the ordinary way my father never found time for a game of any sort, except draughts occasionally. But after the midday meal on Good Friday, and following the custom he was used to as a boy, he would have the kitchen cleared, and we all settled down very happily to a game of marbles.

As to the origin of the custom, the following is a possible suggestion. Good Friday is of course a Holy Day or holiday, and our ancestors of centuries ago had a way of celebrating such occasions in a very noisy fashion, drinking and dancing being much to the fore. The Puritan clergy of the seventeenth century would feel that this was most unseemly on a day commemorating the Crucifixion: they often express that aversion in our own times. But marbles is a quiet, sober sort of game, and they may well have thought that if their parishioners must have some sort of amusement, playing marbles was the least objectionable.

Another game was 'peggy', the same I believe as 'tip cat', though we never used the word. The peggy was made from a cylinder of wood, about five inches long and an inch in diameter. The cylinder was divided into three equal parts, and each end, forming a third of the total length, was then tapered off to form a blunt-nosed cone.

In playing the game, the peggy was laid on the ground and the conical end was hit with a stick. The peggy jumped into the air, and the player then hit it again, driving it as far as he could. The winner was of course the one who had been able to make the longest drive, but the complete game would include six or seven drives. It resembled cricket in being an excellent test of one's ability to co-ordinate hand and eye, and it required only the very simplest of materials. There were however occasional disasters to neighbouring windows.

Under the name 'tip cat' the game is probably of great antiquity. John Bunyan (1628-1688) recalls amongst his sins that he had frequently been guilty of playing tip cat on the Sabbath.

It is many years since I saw boys playing 'trundle', but in its season we played it a great deal. We had an iron hoop about two feet in diameter, and a thin bar of iron with a hook to keep it moving. The opposite end from the hook was set in a piece of wood to form a handle. Once the hoop was moving, a very slight pressure on the hook kept it in motion, and it could be turned to the left or the right by the lightest touch on one side or the other.

It may be that part of the attraction of trundle lay in the accompanying noise. It was continuous and rather pleasant, and gave the operator a certain feeling of importance. He was literally making something move, and the people in the neighbourhood could hear him doing it!

I have used the phrase 'in its season'. I can think of only one sport closely related to climatic conditions, and that is skating. What decided the season for marbles, peggy, tops or trundle? I don't know, but certain it is that if you were to be seen whipping your top at the wrong time of the year, you would be the object of the most withering contempt.

Owing to the cost, real skates never came our way, but dowels were a fair substitute, and the blacksmith would make you a pair for fourpence. He simply took a rectangular bar of iron and with bellows, hammer and anvil bent the ends round to form spikes about three quarters of a inch long. Merely to watch him was almost worth the money. He hammered one of the spikes into the middle of our boot heels, and the other into the soles. We were then equipped, or supposed to be, for the dowel had a habit of coming adrift at the slightest provocation.

Of the team games, football was always popular. We rarely had a proper football, but used a stout leather tube about eight inches long and two inches in diameter. I never knew where these came from. We usually played on one of the patches of waste ground, and if these were all occupied we would play in the street.

We began a game by picking up sides. The two captains would toss up for 'first pick', after which, choosing in turn, they would take first one of us then another until the two sides were complete. Neither captain ever seemed to think much of my merits as a footballer, for I was always one of the last to be chosen.

But I did score a goal once. We were playing soccer, and after a desperate struggle it was half-time, with the score standing at eleven - eleven. (Scoring was very frequent in these games). We changed over and a minute later, by great and unusual luck, I found myself in possession of the ball. It was quite near our own goal posts, consisting of the inevitable coats a few yards apart with a brick on each to keep them in place.

Now only a few minutes before, this had been our opponents' goal and for the moment I had overlooked the trifling circumstance that we had changed over. In a few seconds I had scored, but instead of my success being greeted by the usual loud cheers, the first reaction was one of incredulous silence, followed by derisive laughter from the opposite side. I saw then what I had done. It was, I said, a little mistake that anybody might have made, but it took me a very long time to live the incident down.

In summer we played cricket of course. A favourite pitch for small boys though its length was a good deal less than the regulation twenty two yards, was a rectangular patch, now built on, at the junction of Bentinck Street and Brindley Street. The 'wickets' were chalked on the gable end of Darwell's Vaults, a public house which was the last building on that side of Bentinck Street.

On one occasion I was bowling underhand, with a ball that was smaller than a proper cricket ball, but almost as hard. The batsman and myself would each be about ten years old, and there were no other players. We had one spectator however, a big fellow named Welding whose age would be about sixteen. He was standing six or seven yards away to my left, and there would be an angle of about forty five degrees between the line joining me to the wickets, and that joining me to him.

He began to make very insulting remarks about my bowling, such as: "Kid's game, underarm. Proper cricketers allus bowls overarm, but o'course bein' on'y a kid yer couldn't do it. " This was more than flesh and blood could stand for long, and at length I said with all the dignity I could muster: "I'm only bowling underarm because Walker likes that sort of ball. But I can bowl overarm when I like. Just watch!"

I knew the preliminary movements. I went back a few yards to develop a good run, as I thought a real cricketer would. I swung my arm boldly round, and whoosh! Away went the ball as fast as even I could have wished, but not at all in the direction intended. It hit Welding fair and square on the side of the head, and down he went!

*Runcorn Cricket Club circa 1895*

When with a stone in his sling David felled Goliath, he advanced towards him to follow up his success. I made no attempt to imitate him. Instead, I ran as hard as could be to the friendly shelter of my own back yard. In a few seconds Goliath was on his feet and in full chase but I had a good start, got inside and bolted the gate. I was safe for the moment, but with Goliath only maimed and living in the neighbourhood the risks of leaving him unappeased were obvious. I climbed up the back gate, peered over the top and managed to convince him that he had been the victim of a most extraordinary accident.

For many years I thought this was the case, though the chance of a badly-aimed ball hitting Welding as it did must have been one in many hundreds. It seems more probable to me now that there was a psychological explanation. Consciously I was aiming at the wicket, but subconsciously at the enemy who had been taunting me, and my subconscious aim was remarkably accurate. Luckily I had only the strength of a small boy or the consequences could have been very serious.

Though we followed the normal practice of playing with stumps chalked on a wall, our souls longed for the real thing, with the added refinement of bails. Unfortunately our united capital fell far short of the sum required, so following a common custom we composed a letter headed 'The White Rose Cricket Club', soliciting subscriptions. Of this I remember only the last few words. They remain with me because we had a long discussion as to whether they should be 'the prosperity of the club' or 'the furtherance of the club'. In the end, and in the true British spirit of compromise, we decided on 'the furtherance and prosperity of the club'. Each member of the club then made a copy of the letter and we went round 'subscribing'. At least that was the local term always used, though it hardly fitted the facts, when other people did the subscribing and we did the cadging.

'Subscribing' consisted of knocking at a door, asking the person who opened it "Please to read this" - and hoping. Usually he declined to read it, and even if he did, it was long odds against a halfpenny or a penny being forthcoming. It was uphill work as I recall it, with more kicks than halfpence. I have no clear memory of the result, but we certainly never obtained enough money to buy the stumps. If we had, I should have remembered playing with them. Possibly we collected enough to buy a ball.

Until 1906 there was no swimming bath in Runcorn, but there was one in Widnes, and William and I often spent a pleasant hour there on our way to Farnworth. It was two or three years before we learnt to swim properly, but this did not prevent us from spending most of our time at the six foot end where there was a diving platform. We could swim under water, so we used to dive into the bath diagonally and reach the side, swimming if necessary to supplement the impetus from the dive. Once there, we grasped the horizontal rail and were soon out again to repeat the performance. The time came when we agreed that we ought to learn to swim properly. I was ten and William thirteen, and it did not take us long to learn, chiefly because we were well used to playing about in the water, and this had given us confidence. We had no instruction and acquired no style nor any turn of speed, but we enjoyed ourselves in our own way and both became good 'stayers'.

A little while ago I went to Widnes Baths and found that after more than fifty years it was exactly as I remembered it. The little hot bath is there, just to the right of the entrance. This was a useful substitute for the non-existent bathrooms, and was always a well-populated area, especially on Saturday afternoons. Men from the chemical works used to come for a weekly clean up, and 'mottled blue' soap was provided by the management to assist them in their ablutions. It was so full of soda, it would have removed the skin entirely from anybody not hardened to it.

There was very little room. Only the lucky ones were able to sit on the edge of the bath with both feet inside while behind them it was a case of 'standing room only', a few of the standers having one foot inside. The profanity was unbelievable, the limitations of vocabulary being compensated for by almost infinite repetition. I never heard so much swearing in my life. Perhaps because I was so young, I was nearly always one of the lucky ones to get a look-in. " 'ere, make room for the little b*****" somebody would say, and the little b***** in question was always pleased to accept.

There were no boys of my age in Runcorn who owned bicycles, though a few young men of independent means like Sam and Charlie were proud possessors of 'penny-farthings'. I well remember seeing my first safety bicycle. I was ten or eleven at the time, and I was going with William and my parents to hear Mr Gladstone speak at a political rally some seven miles from Runcorn. We set off to walk, and were half way there when we met a man riding up and down the road on this revolutionary new machine. William and I just stood and stared, lost to everything but the wonder before our eyes. Mother and father carried on, unaware that we were no longer with them. When they realised they had lost us they turned back, but by the time the party was reunited it was too late for the political rally. It grieves me still, that with all the years ahead of me in which to see thousands of safety bicycles, I lost my one and only chance of seeing and hearing the Grand Old Man.

If we had no bicycles, there was an infinite variety of horse-drawn vehicles; carts, traps, and lorries - long flat-bed wagons, some of which had low sides. These provided the means for a delectable pastime. One or more boys would hang on to the tailboard of a cart, or better still heave themselves onto the back of a lorry, so obtaining a free ride which had all the sweetness of stolen fruit. Often this was terminated by a passing spoil-sport who would shout: "Whip be'ind yer cart, Mister, whip be'ind yer cart!" and the uninvited passenger, if wise, would drop off very quickly indeed.

Amusements connected with horse-drawn vehicles were not all of an illicit nature, for occasionally on Whit Monday or Tuesday, or sometimes on a fine Saturday afternoon, there were very pleasant excursions by wagonette. These were often arranged for our church and Sunday school outings, and we much preferred them to the train.

The furthest point would not be very distant, perhaps fifteen miles, and we travelled only slowly, but we had the day before us and what a delightful way of spending it! At eight or ten miles an hour we could really see the countryside. Sometimes when we came to the foot of a steep hill the driver would say "Now, would the gen'lmen please get out and walk a bit, just to ease the 'orses?" So out we would get, and stroll up the hill, keeping pace easily with the wagonette. There were no fast cars to raise the dust, and no heavy transport lumbered past to poison the atmosphere with its stinking fumes. There were no sounds but country sounds, and the lazy drone of insects in the heat and sunshine.

No account of our outdoor amusements would be complete without some reference to 'Runcorn Wakes', a fair which was held annually at the beginning of November on a large patch of waste ground always

*Members of the Holt Family enjoy an outing in a small wagonnette.*
*Larger carriages of this type had facing seats with additional ones on the box beside the driver.*

125

known as The Fairground. There seemed to be patches of waste ground for everything in those days! Here were all the usual coconut shies, shooting galleries and merry-go-rounds, and for a number of years there was even a small menagerie.

I have often heard an old man, Mr Robert Eden, tell of an unpleasant experience which befell him when business took him on a visit to this menagerie. He did a considerable outdoor trade in paraffin oil, and at Wakes time he used to supply stall-holders at the Fair, who used the paraffin for their lamps and flares. On one occasion he was filling up cans at the menagerie when an elephant came nosing round, and though not vicious, he made himself rather a nuisance by poking his trunk amongst the tins of paraffin. Robert gave the trunk a slap, and immediately wished he hadn't, as the elephant started to make for him. Naturally Robert didn't stop to argue the point. He ran with all speed, and managed to get outside the boundary gate just in time.

It is said that an elephant never forgets. Certainly this one didn't. The following November he gave chase as soon as he saw Robert plying his trade inside the menagerie enclosure, and this happened year after year. In fact, it was only by stealthy and indirect means that he was able to supply this particular customer at all.

It was at one of these fairs that I first realised how easily capital can be lost by rash speculation. I was about seven, and William ten. We each had a halfpenny, and for a penny one could have three shies at the Dan Sallies. A single successful shy, and one could choose a toy from a whole selection, each worth a shilling. There could be no doubt about their value, because we had the stall-holder's word for it. Two hits - two toys. Three hits - well, imagination simply boggled. William said afterwards that he explained all this to me, while at the same time pointing out that there was just the faintest element of risk. Perhaps he did. I was so attracted by the wonderful possibilities that I never gave a thought to anything else.

I handed over the halfpenny, and William picked up the three balls. He did his very best, and with ball number two he actually made a Dan Sally shake, but the stall-holder said that didn't count. The venture was a total loss, and it was a very gloomy pair that took a last wistful look at those wonderful toys, every one of them worth a shilling.

The menagerie was always a great attraction at the time, but it rather paled into insignificance when the town was visited by Sanger's Circus. Its arrival was advertised by a sort of triumphal procession, the highlight of which was a silver car drawn by eight lovely white ponies. On this car was a large silver platform, and on the platform a golden throne on which sat a queen with a richly jewelled crown.

We gasped with amazement at the sight of it all, but unfortunately we couldn't stay to contemplate it or we should have been late for afternoon school. We had been specially warned of the dire consequences if this should happen.

There was a special reason for this warning. Sanger's Circus had visited the town four years earlier, and a report had spread like wildfire amongst the schoolchildren watching it that Gaffer Jordan had postponed the opening of school until half past two. As a result, scores of boys arrived three quarters of an hour late. The report they had heard must have originated in wishful thinking, and was not accepted as an excuse. It was a lesson in the importance of obtaining official confirmation; Mr Jordan caned the entire batch of delinquents.

Sanger's was an outside affair, but every Whit Monday we had our own processions. In the morning the Clubs walked: the Oddfellows, Rechabites, Sons of Temperance and a great many others. Each would have its large silk banner with a few descriptive words and probably some symbolic design beautifully worked in glowing colours.

Grouped round it would be the various officers; the Secretary, Treasurer, and so forth, each wearing his badge of office. This was usually a broad silk band passing diagonally over the shoulder and carrying an inscription and design, also in rich colour.

Clubs which could afford it would engage a band, and just as the observer was beginning to lose the last faint notes of 'Swanee River', he might become conscious that the strains of 'Onward Christian Soldiers' were becoming more insistent. The Clubs certainly put up a brave show, making a strong appeal to both eye and ear, but it is many years now since the banners were furled for the last time. A sad loss, these outdoor events which made such a colourful contribution to civic life.

In the afternoon it was the turn of the Sunday schools. This was and still is an impressive show, each school headed by its banner, and many of the scholars carrying flags. (There was always great competition amongst the girls for the honour of holding a banner string). The tiny tots, all dressed in white, were conveyed in carts or lorries.

There used to be much discussion as to whether a 'Church' or 'Chapel' school should lead the procession but the matter was amicably settled by giving each one the lead in alternate years. There was evidently nothing new or peculiar to Runcorn about this rivalry. Forty years before in one of her books, Charlotte Brontë refers to an occasion when 'Chapel' was leading, and there was a very long gap between the rear of their procession and the van of the church procession. As the latter, headed by the rector, came into sight round a bend in the road, 'Chapel' struck up with 'See the mighty host advancing, Satan leading on'!

Enough has been said of the simple amusements and activities of my childhood for it to be plain that children were in no real need of pity on that score. Facilities might be lacking, but the young have a natural genius for enjoyment, which they seem to create for themselves and each other under almost any circumstances.

It is far different for adults, and here the deficiency was great enough to give rise to a serious problem. There was the football match on a Saturday afternoon, and there was cricket in the summer, but there were few other outlets available to the working man of 1890 if he were not involved in the life of the church or had no absorbing hobby.

Apart from the lack of radio and television, few working class houses in industrial areas had gardens, and there were no allotments. Once a man had reached home after a hard day's labour, had his tea and perhaps spent half an hour with the Liverpool Echo, there was nothing in prospect but an evening of boredom in a noisy and overcrowded kitchen. It might be argued that there were books and handicrafts and the means of self-entertainment, but then as now, there was a high proportion of people who were not book-lovers or capable of creative activities, and so were dependent on ready-made amusement.

In my youth there was just one place where it could be found, and that was the pub. The prevalence of drunkenness with all its wretched consequences was not a primary social evil though many regarded it as such. It was the outcome of a society which had too little to offer a man seeking relaxation from long hours of hard and unrewarding toil.

The only other indoor amusement on offer was a theatre at the top of Duke Street known as 'The Blood Tub' because of the gory melodramas

**The Whitsum Walk**

Both the Sunday Schools and The United Order of Oddfellows are on parade.
Father is in a straw hat to the right of the picture.

which were its stock-in trade. It may also have doubled up on occasion as a Music Hall, but I have no certain knowledge on this matter. This probably did something towards filling the void, but it was absolutely taboo to the Nonconformist, a relic no doubt of Puritan tradition.

This tradition dated back two hundred years or more to the reign of Charles the Second. Under the Cromwellian regime which preceded it, all theatres were closed. When they reopened, the pendulum swung to the opposite extreme and the plays were often very licentious.

There was also the popular conviction, sometimes justified, that actresses were ladies of easy virtue. Certainly Nell Gwynn has gone down in history as one of the most famous courtesans, and in Victorian times many well known actresses were 'kept' by members of the aristocracy. Sometimes they even succeeded in marrying them!

Quite understandably, decent minded citizens absented themselves and so the tradition was born that the theatre was not a suitable place of entertainment for respectable people.

As a direct consequence of this attitude I was grown up and living away from home when I saw my first play. The nearest approach to it was a very occasional 'Magic Lantern' show at the Public Hall, and no modern film costing a million pounds could hold me spellbound as did those early 'stills' projected onto a screen. It was the first pale streak of dawn, before the sun rose in this century on the greatest entertainment industry the world had ever seen.

Elections could scarcely be classed as 'entertainment', but when they did come round they were certainly welcome diversions.

The Labour movement in the 'nineties was only a concept, discussed amongst intellectuals in each other's houses. It was the Liberal party which held the working man's allegiance, and Gladstone - The People's William - was his idol. There was a specially close link, because he had been born in Liverpool only twelve miles away and Hawarden, his country home, was in Cheshire.

Second only to him was Sir John Brunner, MP for the Northwich Division of which Runcorn was a part. He was Managing Director of Brunner Mond, a huge chemical concern which later expanded into ICI; a very enlightened man and ahead of his times in his care for his workforce.

His position was impregnable, and as far as anywhere could be said to be rock solid, Runcorn was rock solid for the Liberals.

There was no question of lolling in front of the television to hear the arguments of course. Men - and sometimes their wives - packed the political meetings which were held in halls and in the open air. Oratory was the order of the day, and so was heckling for the hapless Tory candidate who had to win his spurs fighting a hopeless cause if he were to stand a chance at a later date of being offered a constituency with a better hope of success.

There was a great deal of rough-and-tumble, and though of course there were no 'votes for women' they were no less fanatic in their loyalties.

I knew of one old lady who always kept a bucket of water behind her front door at election times.

"Are ye for Brunner?" she would ask suspiciously of any unfamiliar young man who stood smiling on her doorstep. "Well no, I am here on behalf of your Conservative candidate, Mr. . . "

He never got any further. She upped with her bucket and her aim was unerring.

It was a far cry in the 'nineties, but the day was to come when no Liberal candidate was fielded at a general election for the Northwich Division, and for the older generation in Runcorn, it was the end of their political world.

# CHAPTER 11

# Prevention and Cure

It is now thirteen years since the 'Welfare State' came into being, and the free medical and health services that are an integral part of it. During those years the scheme has not been without its critics; it is costing far more than the country can afford - doctors are prescribing expensive medicines when simpler ones would meet the case - nothing free should ever be given to the British because it robs them of their natural spirit of independence - these are only a few of the complaints that are aired in Parliament, in the correspondence columns of newspapers, and by doctors and patients themselves.

It would perhaps restore a sense of proportion if the cavillers could go back seventy years in time and look about them at the babies in the prams and the children in the streets; perhaps even find themselves in need of skilled surgical attention, or one of the range of antibiotics to put a quick end to the horrors of double pneumonia, rather than the death which was so frequently the outcome.

There are not so many people left alive now who saw and experienced these things at first hand. Bonnie youngsters are taken for granted. Everybody has them; just look at that Mrs Jones down on the new housing estate with the fifth expected in the spring, and a husband who never does a day's work if he can help it. Mrs Jones would not have had bonnie babies in 1890. Most that survived the first year of life were pale and sickly-looking, wailing day and night in physical discomfort. Of every thousand babies born in that year, one hundred and fifty one did not survive to see their first birthday.

There were many causes for this state of affairs, the first and most obvious being the lack of any means of contraception, and the large size of families. With so many mouths to feed, this further exacerbated working-class poverty. It is interesting to note however that when such means did become available, it was the upper classes who were the first to adopt them, the idea of family limitation only spreading slowly downwards through society and making no universal impact until the present generation.

Another factor was medical ignorance. Not only was no informed help available to combat the diseases that killed so many children, but theories gained medical approval that positively aided the process.

Early in my parents' married life - long before my day - three of the children were at death's door with an infectious disease, and the accepted treatment for a fever was to deprive the patient of all fluids.

George, who was my eldest surviving brother and was either older than the other two, or less sick or more enterprising, slaked his raging thirst by drinking all the bottles of medicine on the mantelpiece and actually recovered!

Undoubtedly the feeling of helplessness in the face of insuperable odds bred a fatalistic attitude, but religious attitudes which are now largely confined to the Roman Catholic Church would have been much more widespread in 1890. In most religious homes, the birth of large numbers of children and the death of half of them was accepted with resignation as 'The Will of God'. It would have been regarded as a sin, to try and alter by human agency that which had been divinely ordained. In many non-religious homes the convenient removal by natural process of more mouths than could ever be fed was undoubtedly looked upon as a fortunate dispensation.

I still have an old friend in Runcorn, one of the survivors of a large Victorian family. He told me that when he married he had no great wish for a family of his own, because it was one of his abiding childhood memories that there seemed always to be a dead baby in the house.

Many middle-class couples of my own generation reacted in this way and of the marriages that took place during and after the First World War, so many were childless that the situation gave rise to a certain amount of official anxiety. Fortunately however, babies never remain out of fashion for very long.

The risk to the mother of seventy years ago was a very real one. The dangers of childbirth can never be entirely eliminated, but with lack of ante-natal and post-natal care, the chances of infection and the poor facilities for dealing with surgical emergencies, they were far greater then. The maternal mortality rate was one in two hundred compared with the present-day one in two thousand.

My own mother always had a doctor in attendance at her confinements, but this was unusual in working-class households. Except in emergencies, the midwife normally sufficed. This may still be so today, especially in isolated country districts, but the midwife is always qualified both in general nursing and obstetrics.

In Runcorn the profession tended to be hereditary, or at all events to run in families, and no other qualification was needed. One branch of the Holt family had the greatest connection, the torch being handed on from mother to daughter-in-law through three generations. Old Mrs Holt trained the famous Mary Ann, and Mary Ann trained Nellie who did eventually qualify in 1910 under the terms of the new Midwives' Act.

These women, and many like them, were skilled in their work and experienced enough to know when medical help must be sought. Others were the worst type of Sairey Gamp, and the doctor would often be called too late to save some poor baby from mutilation, or the mother from a fatal infection caused by dirty hands.

If the baby arrived safely, its best hope for continued survival lay in nature's own provision of breast feeding. If this failed and a bottle had to be substituted the outlook was bleak, especially if the child had the misfortune to be born in the summer. There were no patent baby foods and it would be weaned onto cow's milk. Possibly this might be watered down, but there would be no other allowance made for the difference between a baby's digestion and that of a calf.

As late as 1911, when my own daughter could not be breast fed, I was sufficiently uneasy about the situation to look up the figures, and was horrified to learn that three-quarters of bottle-fed babies died within the first year.

In the story of milk lies the clue to much of the disease that was rife in the nineteenth century. The shippons in which the cows were milked were often filthy places, and if the farm-hand wiped the udder first with a bit of old sacking, it was his only concession to hygiene.

Between the farmer and the customer there were many other points at which contamination could and did take place. For one thing, the roundsman could not be expected to keep his hands very clean when he had to harness and unharness the horse; he certainly paid no attention to the mourning-bands in his broken fingernails.

There was always sediment at the bottom of the milk jug; suspended fragments probably originating in the cowshed. When it began to assume the proportions of a tilth mother would complain to the roundsman, but this never achieved more than a temporary improvement.

Everyone was dosed at frequent intervals with infected milk, and attacks of summer diarrhoea were accepted as one of the inscrutable dispensations of Providence. Most people gradually built up a resistance of it, unless they had the misfortune to die in the process.

The effect on young babies was much more catastrophic. A severe attack of gastro-enteritis could kill them in a few hours and frequently did. They were given the same unsterilised milk as the rest of the family, and faced the added risk of infection from the type of feeding bottle which was then in vogue. This had a rubber tube about eighteen inches long, the idea being that the child could lie in its pram and take a few consoling sucks whenever it felt like it without any attention from its mother. The tube was almost impossible to clean, and few people made any attempt to do so.

Low standards of cleanliness further increased the dangers of infection. This was largely the result of ignorance, for research on bacteria was still very much at the laboratory stage, and elementary principles of hygiene which every girl now learns at her Secondary School were not then considered necessary even by the general practitioners themselves.

Admittedly there was little scope for individual effort with no water-borne sanitation and every backyard privy a breeding ground for flies, but if it had been known that flies were carriers of disease, problems of sewage disposal could have been tackled years before.

For the same reason, no effort was made to keep flies from food stuffs, so that babies which survived the initial hazards of the milk supply were soon exposed to this further danger. Of those which did survive, few achieved positive health and well being.

There were no clinics or health visitors to give the overworked mother such help and guidance as might have been available. When she could stand the crying no longer, she would probably send an older child to the chemist for a bottle of 'Mother's Comfort', a mixture containing opium or 'laudanum' as it was then known. There was no restriction on the sale of dangerous drugs, and no restriction on the mother's giving the baby as many doses of the medicine as she liked. The wonder is not that so many babies died, but that so many lived.

We hear much today of the danger to youngsters of an over-rich diet. This, so we are told, leads to excessive growth in the early years and to premature adolescence, all of which may result in a correspondingly early onset of degenerative disease.

On that basis, the late Victorian schoolchild would have been regarded as a first-class risk by insurance companies. There were plenty of other obstacles to longevity, but overeating was not one of them. The diet in most working-class homes was inadequate both as to quality and quantity, and there was no possibility of supplementing it with a free issue of vitamins because vitamins had not been discovered.

Most children as I remember them were undersized by present-day standards. A few like William were fine, well-grown lads, but they were the exception. Girls in their teens were so often listless and anaemic, that this was looked upon as a normal stage of development. Vitamins might be lacking, but chemists did a brisk trade in Parrish's Food and Iron Jelloids.

It is difficult for a layman to assess the effect of undernourishment on the spread and virulence of infectious diseases. Overcrowding must have been an equally potent factor, and these were only two of many. One has only to look inside the village church and read the long list of names and ages on the family tomb of the local Squire to realise that the well-to-do were no better able to keep their children alive than the poorest in the parish.

Figures make dull reading, but they bring home the hard fact that in 1890, when the population of the country was little more than half of what it is today, roughly fifty two thousand children died of measles, nine thousand of scarlet fever and seven thousand of diphtheria. This would suggest that the terrible loss of life from these causes in my own family was nothing very unusual.

By the end of the century, great fever hospitals were being built on the outskirts of every town and city in a determined effort to curb the spread of these infections and provide better treatment for the sufferers. They served their purpose, but now after only sixty years the wheel has come full circle, and they are standing almost empty or being put to other uses, so swift and dramatic has been the advance of medicine through the development of new drugs and vaccines in this particular field.

Before we had been long at school, we became well used to the sight of children who were lame or deformed. There were many causes for this, of which rickets was probably the commonest. Improved living standards and vitamin D have now combined to banish the disease, and many of the younger doctors in practice today have never even seen a case.

Babies are often born with malformations, and even more often in the past they suffered injury at birth. If that should happen, there were no special hospitals and orthopaedic surgeons available. The child born with a club foot or congenital dislocation of the hips stayed that way to the end of its life.

Badly-united fractures were another common cause of deformity. Doctors did their best, but in the absence of x-rays and skilled surgery the best was not always good enough.

Worst of all however were the ravages of bovine tuberculosis, which in children and young people commonly affects limbs and joints. The reservoir of infection was of course the dirty milk supply, and here again ignorance was bliss. Many eminent doctors maintained that bovine TB was not the same as the human variety, and in this they were right, but they lightly assumed that humans could not catch the disease through drinking tuberculous milk, and in this they were quite wrong.

Farmers did not hesitate to mix tuberculous milk with the main supply, but I well remember about 1905, talking to a farmer who was not too happy about the situation. He said that sometimes only the milk from a single teat was affected, and he would let this go to waste, but regarded the milk from the other three as saleable. "Many a farmer would sell the whole lot," he said, and no doubt he was right.

Many old folks of my generation look back wistfully to the days when milk was three half pence a pint, when milk tasted like milk and there was no skimming half the cream off it, but we have bought release from a national scourge for the extra sixpence halfpenny.

Few parents paid any attention to defects of sight and hearing. These were far more prevalent than they are now, chiefly because children recovering from infectious diseases didn't receive sufficient after-care.

I remember suffering from earache myself on more than one occasion, and mother was most sympathetic. She didn't believe in the remedy of her childhood days when you put your ear to a keyhole and let the cold wind whistle into it to anaesthetise the pain, because the pain was worse when the effect wore off, but she still didn't regard it as serious. It classed with toothache, - significant only as a pain. Her remedy was a small hot onion pushed into your ear and held there with a stocking tied round your head. It seems almost mediaeval.

I also became very short-sighted at the age of about ten. I was moved to the front of the class, but even then I was only able to see what was written on the board by squinting through one of the eyelet holes in the strap of my satchel. Father thought I ought to have glasses, and took me down to Mr Wilton the chemist. Mr Wilton was in no sense an optician; he simply sold glasses. I tried on pair after pair, reporting better and better results, until at last I pitched on some of almost telescopic power and announced that those were the glasses for me.

"I suppose it's alright," Father said a bit doubtfully to Mr Wilton, "but do you think they might draw 'is eyes?"

"Well there is that," admitted Mr Wilton, "they might draw 'is eyes."

The two experts conferred anxiously on this dire possibility and in the end I had to be content with a weaker pair, but I went away well pleased, because they were a deluxe model. Father had never paid more than one and six for glasses before, and these cost half a crown.

Years afterwards, I found I had quite a complicated form of astigmatism. I certainly remember suffering a great deal from headaches as a child.

The surviving male infants born in the 'nineties were the young men who were called to the colours in the Great War. The army doctors were horrified at their low physical standard, and thousands had to be rejected because they were stunted or deformed, or they were deaf in both ears or blind in one eye. Immediately it became a matter of grave national concern, and the cry went up that we were a C3 nation. It seems odd, that this should have come as a surprise.

So many of the illnesses of childhood were preventable, due as much to social conditions as to lack of medical knowledge. But when serious illness arose, either in childhood or in adult life, how well was the medical profession equipped to deal with it?

138

In one respect, the doctor of yesterday was on equal terms with his counterpart of today. He could make use of the sovereign remedy: "Go to bed and stay there until I tell you to get up. " Unfortunately the doctor of yesterday was at a great disadvantage in all other respects and this applied equally to medicine and to surgery.

In this field, two major diseases have been conquered for which there was then no cure. It was tacitly recognised that a sufferer from either was doomed, and news of a fresh victim of diabetes merely provoked the interested enquiry: "Eatin' or drinkin'?" or in the case of consumption "Gallopin' or ornery?"

Diabetes yielded suddenly and completely in 1921 to Banting's discovery of the insulin treatment. The fight against tuberculosis of the lungs has been slower and less spectacular, a combined operation conducted on several fronts. It is only within the last year or so that the new drugs have achieved a final breakthrough on the grand scale.

'Consumption' as we called it was rampant in 1890, claiming about ninety thousand victims in that year alone. Attempts at treatment were on hopelessly wrong lines. Patients were kept in a rather warm room with the doors and windows tightly shut, the idea being to avoid possible fluctuations of temperature.

The prime causes, as with the infectious diseases of childhood, were malnutrition, overcrowding - and ignorance. An old granny sitting in a chimney corner might be a carrier decimating an entire family. She had had that old cough so long, nobody took any notice of it, and if she were spitting freely they didn't bother about that either. In better-class circles spitting was coming to be looked upon as unrefined, but nobody though of it as dangerous.

It is small wonder that the Victorian romantic novelist disposed of her unwanted heroines by sending them into a 'decline'. The hacking cough and hectic flush were sinister portents, and sure indications that the worst might be expected.

Pneumonia was curable but the death-rate was very high, and convalescence took weeks or even months if complications set in, as they often did. A prolonged illness is an inconvenience now, but it was a disaster before the days of National Insurance. If the father were ill, there would be nothing coming in but a few shillings a week from the Sick Club. The discovery of antibiotics in the late 1930's revolutionised the treatment of pneumonia. Recovery is usual in a matter of days, and it is rarely necessary for a patient to be taken to hospital.

The foundations of modern surgery had already been laid by 1890. Simpson had first used chloroform in 1847, and Queen Victoria had set a new fashion by having it for her confinements. Lister was still alive in 1890, but his great principles of asepsis had long since become standard practice. The horrors of indiscriminate butchery and hospital gangrene were things of the past.

Surgery was possible in theory, but in practice even the simplest operation was regarded as a hazardous undertaking. Twelve years later, in 1902, King Edward VII developed acute appendicitis on the eve of his coronation, and the medical profession itself took the gloomiest possible view of his chances. Runcorn was all prepared for the great day with a full programme of entertainments and a great bonfire waiting to be lit on the Hill, so when the blow fell they were anxious to know whether the arrangements should be cancelled or merely postponed. They took counsel of Dr McDougall, the Medical Officer of Health, and he was in no doubt at all, giving it as his opinion that "the King will surely die."

The King did not die, but he had Royal luck. Compared with the present day, surgical instruments were crude, and surgical techniques in their infancy. There were no X-rays, so that the task had to be undertaken without complete investigation.

If haemorrhage had occurred, his life could not have been saved with a blood transfusion; these had been tried years before and abandoned. Nothing was known of blood groups, and doctors were unable to explain why sometimes a blood transfusion was successful, but more often the patient died.

On the credit side of the ledger, what positive achievements were there to record?

Real progress had been made in Public Health, though there was still a long way to go. Open sewers had been filled in; streets were kept clean and were properly surfaced. Towns even the size of Runcorn had a piped water supply, and one that was free from contamination.

The great cholera epidemics of which Runcorn had had its share, were a thing of the past. (There is an interesting reference to one of particular severity in the diary of the same William Holt who co-founded the first Sunday school over thirty years before. He wrote: 'At Runcorn, the afternoon of the 11th of October 1832 was set apart for thanksgiving to God for the removal of the cholera').

Typhus, a disease bred in filth, was virtually extinct, and the incidence of typhoid was greatly reduced, the germ which caused it having been identified and isolated in 1880. Smallpox had been conquered. Pock-marked faces were still common, but when mistresses were advertising for servants they no longer added the proviso 'only girls who have had the smallpox need apply'. My mother had a mild attack of it when she was a young girl, and always found this a valuable asset when looking for a situation.

Vaccination was compulsory, but when I was a baby it was 'from arm to arm'. In the doctor's surgery there would be some babies who had been vaccinated a few days before and whose arms, if the vaccine had taken, were at the sore stage. There would also be a few others waiting to be treated.

Selecting a healthy-looking one from the first group, the doctor would take a little of the lymph from its arm to vaccinate babies of the second group. It occasionally happened that the donor baby was not really healthy after all, so that some undesirable infection was transmitted with the lymph.

So much achieved - so much still to do. Yet the country was on the threshold of great things, and of all the scientific discoveries that have wrought such changes in my own life span, none are more significant to me that those which have conferred longer life and better health on those who seventy years ago had little prospect of either.

Though Runcorn could do nothing to hasten the advent of an X-ray machine, a cottage hospital was a more immediate possibility and a very desirable one. It was an industrial town, and accidents in the chemical works and tanneries were frequent. As things were, a man having a serious accident which required specialist or surgical attention had to be taken to Liverpool, and the journey was not only painful, but liable to aggravate the injury. When his relatives and friends wished to visit him, they had the inconvenience and expense of this same twelve mile journey. It was obviously much better that a patient should receive treatment in Runcorn, and when necessary a surgeon be brought in from Liverpool.

The difficulty was the cost, but beginning in 1895, Runcorn started to 'save up'. The great local effort of the year was the torchlight Bicycle Parade. Though the core of this consisted of bicycles dressed up in all sorts of ways, there were many other features. The procession was usually led by the Volunteer Band, and at a good distance behind - so far away that its competing 'music' would not clash, was the 'Blue Hungry Band'. Its name was a skit on the famous Blue Hungarian Band which was hitting the headlines at the time.

It was constantly hungry for any proper musical instruments beyond a tin whistle or a mouth organ; every household article that could be hit with a stick to make a noise - bucket, shovel or washboard - was pressed into service. There was of course a Queen, enthroned on a lorry and surrounded by her maids of honour, all dressed in white and decked out in flowers. The various works of the town also competed for the best tableau, and these too were mounted on lorries. They were drawn by fine Shire horses, a type now almost extinct. Collectors were everywhere. Just as they do in carnivals today, they would raise their bags on the end of long poles to the bedroom windows, and gather a rich harvest from people watching the fun.

Besides taking a very active part in the Parade, the men in the local works made small regular weekly contributions, and after many years of such effort, and aided by generous gifts from some of the wealthier citizens, the object was finally achieved and the hospital was opened in 1904.

I would like now to introduce you to the Runcorn doctors familiar to me as a child. They had to work without many of the aids which we now take for granted, but none could have made better use of such resources as they had.

I knew three of them quite well, and when I think of Dr Robinson, who was our family doctor, it occurs to me that there are not so many 'characters' about now as there were when I was young. The present day tendency is for men to be groomed to their profession; they conform to a pattern.

In that respect at all events, nobody could have accused Dr Robinson of conforming to anything. He might have stepped out of Dickens. I suppose his clothes must have been new at one time, but even a child could not help noticing that greenish tinge which is the invariable sign of sartorial old age.

## The 'May Queen'

*Lily Shaw, the first ever 'May Queen' of the Runcorn Bicycle Parade, with her attendants.*
*She later married Spencer Hayes, the locally celebrated tenor.*

He had very prominent blue eyes, and when he walked it was with his feet set wide apart and almost at right angles to each other. I say 'when', because he was usually driven in a trap by a youth of about fifteen who looked almost as odd as the doctor. Skilful driving must have been required, for the ancient pony pulling the trap was reputed to be blind.

The doctor used a rather large, battered old leather case which had a special interest for me because it was in this case, so I was given to understand, that a new baby sister had been brought to our house.

There was nothing unprofessional about Dr Robinson's assistant, Dr Binks. He had gravitas. He brought to the bedside that measured, reassuring air which was just right. He pursed his lips as each symptom was described and nodded his head from time to time with a slow, significant nod. When he did emit an occasional "Ah," or "Hmm," one sensed the weight of medical knowledge and experience that lay behind the utterance. With Binks in charge, there was no need for further worry.

Years later I discovered that he was unqualified, and the 'doctor' merely a courtesy title. He must have been almost the last survivor of that earlier generation of apprentices who were allowed to carry out routine treatment under qualified supervision.

My first really close acquaintance with Dr Robinson dates from the time that I was five, so the year would be 1889. By a strange coincidence, William and I had both been losing sleep from aching back teeth; the offending molars would have to be extracted. There was no dentist in those days. The alternatives were the chemist who charged sixpence, or the doctor who charged a shilling. Father magnanimously decided on a shilling's worth for both of us, and arranged with Dr Robinson that we should attend his surgery at six o'clock on a certain evening.

I remember looking forward to the engagement with the most joyful anticipation, and I must have wearied the entire household with my repeated enquiries as to whether it was not yet six o'clock. It was no use them all telling me that it hurt to have a tooth out; I just did not believe them. Nothing would shake my conviction that a most delightful experience lay before me. Whether William shared my views I cannot remember. We set off together for the surgery, and when our turn came he claimed, a bit unfairly I thought, the right of seniority to have his tooth out first.

Even for a shilling one cannot expect everything, and the terms did not allow for an injection or for gas, even if such luxuries had been available. The method employed was an honest, straightforward pull and this was accompanied by a most blood-curdling yell from William. I must have been slightly puzzled, but the strange thing is that I still looked forward to my turn. I cannot understand why this should have been so after hearing William's yell; I simply record the fact. Certainly the deep-seated belief was destroyed a minute later, finally and for ever.

I have a very happy recollection of the last time I had any personal contact with Dr Robinson. I was twenty one, and about to enter University College, Nottingham. It was necessary to produce a certificate of medical fitness, so I made my way to his surgery. I was the first arrival. After a minute or two he opened the door of his consulting room and asked me in. I explained my errand.

He did the usual routine checks, then "What about your sight?" he asked. I told him that I was short-sighted, but could see perfectly well with glasses. (I can't remember whether I was still wearing the famous half-crown pair, but probably not).

Just then we could hear somebody entering the waiting room. The doctor opened the door and asked the patient to come in. Turning to me he said: "This is a man I am treating for ear trouble. I can deal with him and test your sight at the same time." He made the man sit down and turn his head sideways. Then into the ear he slipped an instrument something like a very short silver trumpet. "Now look down there," he said, "and tell me what you see." I did as well as I could and was soon greeted with "Capital, capital. Not much wrong there;" he then presented me with the required certificate.

Perhaps it was because I was so very interested in this odd examination that I quite forgot to ask him what his fee was, and I didn't remember it for some days by which time I was already in Nottingham. I wrote at once, apologising for my forgetfulness and asking him to send me his bill. I have often wished I had kept his reply. Scrawled across my own letter in big writing were the words:

*Dear Son,*
*Glad to have been of use. Couldn't think of accepting a penny.*
*John Robinson*

*Dr. Robinson*

*H.F. Starkey*

If the old chap's coat was green with age it was not from meanness. I have often heard my father say it was difficult to get him to send in a bill, and when after much prodding one did arrive, he was sure that the amount was not a half of what he really owed.

In those days of course there was not even a forerunner of the National Health Service, but most workmen would belong to the local branch of their Union (Shipwrights', Boilermakers' or whatever it might be), which would include a Sick Club. Many of them would also be a member of a Friendly Society, such as the Grand United Order of Oddfellows or the Lily of the Valley Lodge, which also allowed benefit. The Club or Friendly Society would arrange with a doctor to attend its members for a fixed annual sum, and this would include the cost of medicines. A member would receive sick pay of twelve shillings a week for a certain number of weeks, after which the pay was reduced by stages to four shillings, remaining constant at that level as long as the member remained 'on the Club'.

The doctor for father's club was McDougall, and so it was that McDougall always attended him although Robinson was our family doctor.

When he was fifty, father became ill with pernicious anaemia, a complaint about which little was then known. It still cannot be cured, but it can be kept completely under control by a monthly injection of vitamin B12. Unfortunately, this discovery - and the original simpler but much less pleasant remedy of eating raw ox liver - came too late for father. When the disease was diagnosed by a specialist in Liverpool he was told that his expectation of life was two years. In fact, his iron constitution kept him alive for nine, and he had 'remissions' when he seemed comparatively well. Except for those times, he was on the Club for the whole nine years, and it was usually my job to go to the surgery for his medicine. In this way I got to know Dr McDougall quite well.

He once told father with satisfaction that a few days previously he had cured the most difficult case he had ever been called upon to treat. Naturally father wanted particulars and Dr McDougall explained. The patient complained of back pain, and it seemed that no treatment could bring about any improvement. Then the doctor heard that this man was insured in three clubs, and instantly became suspicious. However, he couldn't prove that it was a case of malingering and the situation dragged on unchanged for many weeks.

At last he had an idea. "This is a very obstinate case," he said, "but I am going to try heat treatment, which sometimes works wonders. I want you to strip to the waist." The patient did so, and Dr McDougall arranged a broad strip of brown paper along the man's spinal column. Then he brought in an ordinary flat iron which had been heated. "It will hurt a bit," he said, "but you mustn't mind that. Just remind yourself that you are now being cured of that horrible backache." With this, he began ironing vigorously over the brown paper. The man wriggled violently, mopped his brow, swore now and then to relieve his feelings and finally declared that he could stand it no longer. "But you must," said the doctor. "The heat is drawing out the pain wonderfully. You have only had two minutes of the treatment and it may need another ten." More ironing, more protests. Soon the man agreed that the pain was a little better. "Splendid," said the doctor, "however, we must keep on until the pain has gone altogether. But this iron is cooling a bit. Just wait a minute while I change it for a freshly-heated one."

When he returned, flourishing flat iron number two, the surgery was empty. The cure had evidently been complete, and events proved that it was not only complete, but lasting. Father enquired several times, but Dr McDougall never had to report the return of the patient for further treatment.

Dr McLennen was considerably younger than Robinson and McDougall. I remember him chiefly in connection with the 'Volunteers', the predecessors of the Territorials. He was medical officer to the Runcorn company, and I can see him now in his smart officer's uniform, bringing up the rear when they were out on parade, red coats and gold-braided trousers all complete. In front would be the brass band, helping them all to keep time with a vigorous rendering of Colonel Bogey.

Doctors may not in general be a very long-lived race, but all our Runcorn doctors made old bones. Drs Robinson and McDougall both passed the eighty mark, while Dr McLennen reached the age of ninety three and died only a short time ago.

It seems clear that if a doctor wishes to live a long time, he should either walk his rounds as did two of them, or alternatively drive a blind pony.

# CHAPTER 12

# Out and About in Runcorn

As with most other English towns, the greatest changes in Runcorn have taken place at the perimeter. New housing estates have sprung up on the outskirts, and surrounding villages like Halton and Weston are losing their separate identity and becoming suburbs, joined to the parent town by an umbilical cord of small modern houses flanking the main roads. These roads were once just lanes, with a prospect from every field gate of deep pasture, and in the autumn of ripe corn waiting to be carried.

Until three or four years ago, the 'hard core' of Runcorn remained almost unaltered. The principal streets, the canal bridges, the public buildings and even many of the shops were much as I remembered them. The Bridgewater canal running through its centre is still the dominant feature of the town as it was in my time and for a century before that, but great changes have come at last. With the need to provide adequate approaches to the new road bridge being built across the Mersey, the demolition squads are hard at work. Much of the old property in Church Street has vanished and at least half of Lowland Road has gone, bringing Sam Bazley's self-contained little world perilously near to the edge of a much larger one.

But even four years ago, the everyday scene would have been much different from that of 1890. Clothes alone would partly have accounted for that. Take the average schoolboy for instance. His 'short' trousers came to below his knee and covered the tops of his long stockings. Lace-up boots rather than shoes were his usual footwear. If he wore a jacket instead of a jersey it would button up to his neck, and his collar would be of the starched 'lantern' variety. Sometimes a rubber substitute was used for the collar, which though easy to clean was hot and uncomfortable to wear, especially in summer.

The girls' frocks were long enough to cover the tops of their high-laced boots. Often they were old and shabby - sometimes even dirty -

but the poorest mother took pride in the clean starched pinafore with a frilled yoke which was always worn over the top.

Changes in men's fashions are notoriously slow, but the cut of the average suit of 1890 would strike quite an ultra-modern note since its espousal by today's Teddy Boys. Trousers were narrow and had no turn-ups; jackets were long with high lapels. The only difference was that they were worn by the sober and middle-aged as well as by the young, and there were many variations of detail. Collars were stiff, and so tall that they almost propped the chin up, while the fashionable headgear was a 'bowler' with a rather shallow crown.

And watch-chains were worn! A man's status in life could almost be assessed by his watch-chain; whether it was silver or gold, with few or many seals attached, and whether the figure it adorned was lean or prosperous. Fat men were common, and fatness was looked upon by all but the medical profession as a sign of material wealth and physical well-being. It was intended as a compliment if one man were to tell another he was "Looking splendid - fat as a pig!"

No young woman today, even for the sake of eccentricity, would be likely to adopt the feminine fashions of the 'nineties. Dresses were so long that they had to be held up a little by the wearer if they were not to trail on the ground. Should this happen, the dress was protected by a hem of 'brush braid' which projected just a little beyond the edge. No doubt the street-sweepers found their labours eased somewhat by the prevailing mode!

The dress could only appear to advantage if the wearer had the fashionable 'wasp-waist' which was achieved by tightly-laced corsets. This was by no means universal, but it was usual amongst girls who took a pride in their appearance. Though malnutrition was probably a more potent factor, the highly-compressed waist may well have been an additional cause for the anaemia and 'chlorosis' so common amongst young women in the eighteen-nineties.

Strict rules for mourning were observed by most women. For near relations it was a year in unrelieved black, followed by a year's half-mourning in purple or mauve. Widows wore veils whenever they appeared in public, and some remained permanently in black.

This was partly in imitation of Queen Victoria who never ceased to mourn her beloved Albert for the forty years that she survived him, but there was the cynical suggestion that continued mourning had a more practical purpose; it indicated to the world at large that the lady was still unattached and available to offers!

There were no dress shops in the modern sense of the word, and no 'ready-mades' for sale. Drapers such as Morris's and Bowyer's sold material by the yard, and customers had it made up in the workrooms, which were usually above the business. Next to 'service', dressmaking probably absorbed more of the female labour force than any other occupation.

Girls on leaving school served a three-year apprenticeship, after which they might graduate to be head of a workroom, or set up in a separate business and perhaps take on apprentices of their own. Many continued with this work as a side-line, even after marriage.

By way of a postscript to the fashion world of my youth, I recall the story of a distant relative who was clearing out a big room at the top of her house, once the scene of a flourishing dressmaking business of which she had been the head. The 'model' - known locally as a 'toddy' - was a problem, with its prominent bust, minute waist and repository for the once-fashionable bustle. Difficult to dispose of, and anyway she was a woman to whom waste was a sin.

"Albert," she called over the banisters, "take this down to Morris's and see what they'll give you for it. "

Now Albert was a youth reared to habits of obedience, otherwise it seems certain that the commission would have been refused. He set out with his burden and, ignoring the amused glances of passers by, arrived at his destination. There, to his dismay, he found that Morris's had no use for the mannequin either. He was soon back on the street with his unwelcome companion, but had retraced his steps no farther than the point where Savage's Bridge crossed the Bridgewater canal when his spirit rose in revolt. Leaning over the parapet, he launched the headless torso upon its final journey, leaving it to bob away into history on the slowly moving current.

Make-up was unusual in the 'nineties, and a girl who went in for it would be looked upon as 'no better than she should be'. This is rather curious, as the Princess of Wales, afterwards Queen Alexandra, was known to make great use of it.

There may be a simple explanation. In an age much more strongly Puritan than the present, virtue in a woman was a material asset. If she

*Bill Posters at work on the approach to Savage's Bridge, 1891*

H.F. Starkey

wished to marry well, there must be no breath of suspicion regarding her character. For this reason she would eschew make-up, and if she ever smoked a cigarette she would be careful never to be seen doing so in public. For the same reason, respectable women didn't go into public houses.

Not only would the people look different to the visitor from 1959. His attention would soon be attracted to the streets themselves, and the way in which they were surfaced. They were 'macadamised', the name commemorating the Scotsman, R. L. Macadam (1756-1836) who successfully devised this method of construction.

A layer of broken stone six or eight inches deep was spread over the road foundation. This was covered with earth, which was watered freely and rolled into the stone with a steam-roller. The water-bound surface stood up well enough to the comparatively light, slow traffic of those days, but was quite unsuited to modern conditions. So with the turn of the century it gradually gave place to the tarmac surface familiar today. It has to be admitted that not all changes are for the worse. The clouds of dust in dry weather were a most unpleasant feature of the old roads.

Stones often became detached from the water-bound surface, and in my young days stone-throwing was common when two boys or groups of boys had some little difference to settle. It sounds terribly dangerous, but I never myself remember anybody being injured, or even hit. Now and again there would be a crash of glass, but no matter how quickly the irate householder might rush out, he was never in time to see more than the heels of a few boys disappearing round the nearest corner.

In the absence of cars, roads were far safer than they are today. Mothers could and did send their children to school or on errands, feeling that the chances of an accident were so small as to be not worth worrying about. The general speed of horse-drawn traffic would be, at a guess, from six to ten miles an hour. Bicycles of course were faster, and one read occasionally of a cyclist being fined for 'scorching'. Even so, it is unlikely that the offender's speed on the bicycle of those days was anywhere near the thirty miles an hour regarded as safe nowadays.

Now and again one would see a street, or part of a street, covered for a length of twenty or thirty yards with 'tan-bark', a product of the local tanneries. This was a sure sign that somebody was seriously ill, for the bark greatly reduced the noise of passing traffic.

The lighting of streets in the 'nineties was much below present-day standards. Although the incandescent gas-mantle was on the market, the Runcorn street-lamp was still furnished only with the old fashioned 'fish-tail' burner, and the light did little more than make darkness visible. All the same, 'lighting-up' was something of an event with us youngsters. The lamplighter was a Mr Austin, and a group of us would follow him round from lamp to lamp. We would watch him raise his lighting-pole, equipped with a small hook for turning on the gas-tap, and a moment later we cheered as the little flame leapt into life. Then, followed by his faithful band of satellites Mr Austin would move onto the next gas-lamp and favour us with a repeat performance.

Street-cries have almost died out now. Even the rag-and-bone man transacts his business confidentially at the back door. Not so in 1890. His cry of "Rags and bones" was usually extended to include "Shoes and rabbit skins," and he plied a brisk trade. There seemed to be no lack of these commodities amongst a working class that possessed little else. He would give a few coppers in exchange, or a huge lump of salt if his customer preferred it.

There was the strange call "Sampion, sampion," (for samphire). This was a seaweed gathered somewhere in the estuary of the Mersey. It was boiled, and then one could suck the fleshy portion from the central sprig, like a maritime version of asparagus. With a little vinegar it tasted very good indeed, but it went off the market many years ago. It was thought likely to be infected with sewage, and no doubt it was.

Once a year, on the day before Good Friday, quite a different cry was heard, "One a penny, two a penny, hot cross buns!" Vendors we never saw at any other time would come round with shallow trays of the buns, covered with a white cloth. There would be no lack of customers if they could advertise such prices today!

I wonder when the town crier ceased to operate, other than as a 'bygone' resurrected for some special occasion? He would stand with his bell at one strategic point after another, announcing the loss of some item of value, sometimes even a child. I remember one occasion when he cried the loss of a gold sovereign somewhere in High Street or Church Street, and as there was a reward of five shillings for its recovery, I spent about two hours in a diligent search for it, but I regret to say without success.

About five or six o'clock in the evening the newsboy would be calling the Liverpool Echo, with a brief lurid summary of its more startling contents. A typical call might be: ".Liverpool Echo - Special Edition - 'Orrible murder in Bootle - Man arrested." At frequent intervals his calls would cease while he supplied a customer, then the litany would be resumed. The newsboy was all in favour of 'orrible murders'. They provided a wonderful stimulus to his evening sales.

Though they cannot be classed as a street cry, no account of old Runcorn as it fell upon the ear would be complete without some mention of clogs. They were the commonest if not the universal wear amongst the labouring classes, particularly the women. The clatter to work at six in the morning would have awakened the dead and even one bent old woman with a grey woollen shawl over her head could be heard a street away, the flags ringing under her feet.

It is quite surprising, after nearly seventy years, to find the number of shops still trading under the old names. There are Britland the greengrocer, Mack the stationer and Percival the pork butcher to name only a few. Besides the private traders, several branches of the 'Co-op' still occupy their former positions. My cousin Walter Collier, the younger brother of the Francis Collier who later made his name in Methodism, was the proprietor of several grocers' shops. He was a great rival of the Co-op, and one of his best known slogans was: 'Which will win, Collier's low prices or the Store's dividend'?

On one occasion he had a black 'mourning board' placed in front of the window of each of his shops, and people were soon asking if somebody connected with the business had died. "No, it isn't that," was the reply, "but the Store's divi' has just dropped a penny, and Mr Collier has had the boards put up to commemorate the sad event. " The town chuckled over the little joke for the rest of the day.

Incidentally, the Store's divi' was much higher than it is today. At one time it was as much as three shillings in the pound.

Every town has its shops and streets and people going about their business; Runcorn would be little different in this respect from other towns of the same period. It did possess, however, a rather unusual feature in its two canals, both of great importance to the economic life of the locality and both famous beyond their immediate confines though for different reasons.

***Bridgewater Canal - Top Locks***

*Barges and narrowboats are much in evidence. Leinster Gardens is a few minutes' walk away to the left.*

Citizens of Runcorn were so used to the presence of the Bridgewater canal connecting their town with Manchester that they took little notice of it, but a stranger would have found many points of interest. The cargoes of up to sixty tons were carried by barges or 'flats' as we used to call them. Sometimes, instead of a barge, there would be two narrow boats, tied side by side. Both flats and narrow boats were sixty or seventy feet long.

The difference between these two types of boat was not just one of width. The barges were sombre, unlovely things and strictly utilitarian. They worked the length of the Bridgewater canal, and were sufficiently robust to navigate the Mersey, but they were too wide to pass through the narrow locks found elsewhere on the inland waterways. The narrow boats on the other hand, could travel over the whole of the inland waterway system and were definitely eye-catching. The living quarters were partly raised above the level of the deck, with lace curtains to the tiny windows. Their outside panels were gaily painted with traditional designs, in which roses and castles were always the predominant theme. Sometimes as the boats went by, one managed to get a tantalising glimpse of the cosy interior of a cabin, with its brightly coloured china and shining brass and copper.

The flatman lived on board with his family. They all wore clogs, and the man would be clad in the thick blue jersey and trousers which seem to be inseparable from life on the water. His wife would have skirt and bodice of some brightly-coloured striped material, with an equally colourful apron tied round her waist. She was of such circumference as to give the impression of an almost indefinite number of petticoats lurking beneath the skirt, but it may be that the foundations were of a more solid nature. Certainly her more-than-ample waistline sounded a note of defiance to the wasp waist so fashionable at the time.

For headgear she favoured a scarf or shawl, also brightly coloured. As a result of constant exposure to the weather her face was always tanned a rich mahogany brown, and this combined with her fondness for large gold earrings gave her a gypsy-like appearance.

She joined with her husband in doing her full share of the heavy work. The boats were normally towed by powerful draught horses, but sometimes it was necessary to manhandle them through a difficult stretch. At one point just beyond Preston Brook where some high land has to be negotiated, the canal runs underground for more than a mile. The wife or children would lead the horse over the top while the boatman 'legged' the boat through the low tunnel. He lay on a plank or planks covering part of the superstructure of the boat and drove it along by pushing against the roof with his feet.

Just occasionally a horse would fall into the canal while towing. As a youngster I never had the good luck to see this happen, but I knew of the procedure adopted. The tow-rope would be disconnected, and the frightened horse would be encouraged to swim along to one of the points on the canal bank arranged for such an emergency. Here the height of the bank would have been reduced by two feet or so by removing the large coping stones, and with some help from the flatman the horse would get a grip with his front legs and struggle out.

Instead of using a horse for towing, a tug was sometimes employed, but in that case it would be pulling a string of barges with a flatman on each one manipulating the tiller.

One excitement which came all too rarely was the appearance of the 'Sally Ice Boat'. The normal flow of traffic was usually sufficient to keep the waterway open, but occasionally in times of severe frost the ice would become so thick that the boats could not break through. That is, none except the Sally Ice Boat. She was shaped like a punt, maybe four feet wide and thirty feet long, and she was so built that the gunwale was at the waist-level of a man standing in her. Her heavy timbers were clad with iron, and handrails inside ran the full length of her.

With five or six powerful boat horses hitched to the tow-rope and as many stalwart 'boaties' on board as could be accommodated, Sally would charge forward as fast as the horses could run while the crew rocked violently from side to side. It was a thrilling sight, and everybody shouted and cheered as she struck the unbroken ice, which usually gave way at the first assault. Then there was a retreat and the action was repeated until the canal was once more open to traffic.

We were rather proud of our Bridgewater Canal, partly because it was the oldest really large canal in the country. It owed its construction to the third Duke of Bridgewater (1736-1803). He owned large collieries at Worsley and he needed to be able to transport his coal cheaply the eight miles to Manchester, so he had a canal constructed between the two towns. The scheme was so successful that he decided to extend the canal to Runcorn, and the whole of the forty miles of waterway was completed in 1772.

His engineer was James Brindley (1716-1772), who though almost illiterate must have possessed real native genius, for he had been trained as a wheelwright, not as an engineer. He made no drawings and was unable to set out his calculations on paper but they all worked out correctly; his instinct seemed unerring.

Those were long before the days of Runcorn's industrial development. The town possessed a mineral spring and had something of a reputation as a health resort and beauty spot. The Duke liked it so much that he built himself a large Georgian mansion, so situated that he could see his canal with its elaborate system of locks and also command a fine view of the Mersey, at the point where it was broadening out to make its final North Westerly sweep towards Liverpool and the Irish Sea.

There was also a sharp bend in the river at this point which gave the twin towns their names - Widnes was the Wide Nose and Runcorn was the Roomy Cove.

The mansion is still in existence and still known to many as the 'Duke's House', but it ceased years ago to be used a residence and was converted into business premises for the Canal Company.

The locks on the Bridgewater Canal formed two wonderful flights; Top Locks near Leinster Gardens and Bottom Locks near the Duke's House, where the canal entered the River Mersey. This allowed access to the docks which were crammed with small schooners, the biggest ships able to navigate so far up the river. They discharged their cargoes into warehouses or on to the quay, and the barges and narrow boats were loaded up until, deep in the water, they entered the series of locks and progressed slowly up, step by step, until the high level of the canal was reached at Waterloo Bridge.

We youngsters were always fascinated by the locks, whether they were busy or idle. The rush and turmoil of the water as the lock was filling, or the spurts and fountains from the cracks in the gates when it was empty, were a never-failing attraction. But they were dangerous places for children and we were never allowed to go too near. Many a man lost his life crossing the lock gates on a dark and foggy night, taking a short cut on his way back home from the pub.

*Runcorn Docks crowded with schooners, 1886*

H.F. Starkey

The commonest cargo for the narrow boats was china clay for the Potteries, reached via the Trent and Mersey Canal, which connected with the Bridgewater Canal at Preston Brook, five miles from Runcorn. They often came back loaded with crates of crockery bound for the docks. By contrast, the barges worked to Manchester and usually carried huge bales of raw cotton. They collected these from ocean going ships at the port of Liverpool, and when the tide was high enough steam tugs could be seen towing strings of these barges along the Mersey. They always seemed to return 'light' after discharging their cargo.

A common export from Runcorn was sulphuric acid from the chemical works. It was transported in huge carboys and just occasionally there would be an accident, and the flatman would find concentrated acid flowing over him from the broken container. Following a well-recognised and very effective procedure, he would promptly jump into the canal. He would then catch hold of a friendly boat-hook extended to him by his wife, and would soon be on board again, wet through and usually swearing freely, but saved from the terrible injuries the acid would have caused.

The canal's great days are over now. One of the parallel lines of locks is completely disused and in process of being filled up with earth and rubble. Doubtless the other will soon go the same way.

Barges and narrow-boats are few and far between, except in pools and backwaters where scores of them are lying derelict and rotting away. The decline really began many years ago with the construction of the Manchester Ship Canal, which provided a competing water-route between Liverpool and Manchester. But the final blow was struck by road transport. The fact that this can convey loads at thirty or forty miles an hour compared with the three miles an hour of the barge, more than makes up for the heavier running costs.

Unlike the Bridgewater Canal, the Manchester Ship Canal does not go right through Runcorn but merely skirts it. It was begun in 1887 and completed in 1894 so in 1890 the work was in full swing. I well remember all the machinery and equipment assembled at the site. There were queer-looking engines pulling wagon-loads of earth on temporary railways; cranes were everywhere and the sound of pile-driving went on incessantly. Thousands of navvies were employed on the site and a rough lot they were. There was a regular little township of wooden huts near the diggings where they lived.

*The building of the Manchester Ship Canal*

H.F. Starkey

1890 was a year of disaster for those in charge of the undertaking, as may be appreciated from the following excerpt, quoted by permission of the publishers of the Encyclopaedia Britannica; 'In January the work of months was destroyed by flood in a single night, and in November of the same year even worse befell. Storms were added to floods; six miles of the excavated bed were in parts forty feet below water. Steam navvies, locomotives, workmen's tools, plant and material of every kind were submerged. In places the tips of cranes could be seen only a few inches above water. Bridges and temporary erections were overthrown, and the slopes of the canal were washed away in long stretches'.

I still recall people talking of this or that aspect of the disasters wrought by storm and flood; the head-shakings and the atmosphere of gloomy fear that it would never be possible to finish the work. But the construction of the canal was a matter almost of life and death to Manchester. The Corporation put up extra money and in spite of everything the project was carried through to a successful conclusion, though at a cost of sixteen instead of the estimated four and half million pounds.

The creeping paralysis that has overtaken the Bridgewater Canal has had no counterpart here. Ocean-going ships carrying cargoes of every sort can sail right up to Manchester without off-loading at Liverpool, and the city instead of sinking into comparative obscurity has become a prosperous inland port.

Runcorn itself was greatly affected by the construction of the Ship Canal and the results which followed it. While the work was in progress, the presence of many officials and thousands of workmen provided a great stimulus to trade, but when these departed, depression followed. One would have expected this to be purely temporary but unfortunately, even though it now boasted deep water facilities and a lay-by for unloading the tall ships which were unable to pass beneath the railway bridge, Runcorn would never again be the busy canal port of former years.

Prosperity returned at last, though of a different sort. The chemical industry has been an uninterrupted success story since amalgamations and a huge expansion programme has brought I. C. I. into being as one of the greatest chemical combines in the World, its tentacles extending all over Northern England.

Tanning, the other staple industry, has fared less well since the last war owing to the competition from plastic which has reduced the demand for sole leather, but even so Runcorn is at least as thriving today as it was in the 1890's. [Walter didn't live to see the mushroom-growth of the New Town which has changed the employment picture again, with the diversified light industries which have sprung up on the new trading estates].

The new road bridge now under construction between Runcorn and Widnes will no doubt bring further prosperity to the town. Apart from the Mersey tunnel at Liverpool, it will be the lowest point on the river at which road traffic can cross from Cheshire into Lancashire. But it will be a different sort of prosperity, based on bustle, speed and noise. We oldsters do our best to keep up with the times, but we cannot help sighing a little nostalgically for those quieter days associated with flatmen in blue jerseys, their wives in brightly-coloured dresses and the leisurely progress of the horse-drawn barge.

# CHAPTER 13

# Social and Economic Changes

Any fine day towards the end of the last century, knots of men were always to be seen standing about on Savage's Bridge, exchanging bits of gossip or simply leaning idly over the railings and spitting into the water. They may be there still, but not with the pinched faces, ragged clothing and broken-toed boots that I remember. They were out of work, and there was no unemployment pay.

The 'nineties were a period of local depression and the incidence of unemployment was probably higher than in the country as a whole, but if it had been a time of prosperity, seasonal or temporary unemployment would have accounted for many more men than were lounging on Savage's Bridge. Should the canal be frozen over, or the weather so wet that work had to be discontinued on a building site, the best that the workman and his family could expect was near starvation on Parish Relief. These conditions were not peculiar to Runcorn, but applied equally to any other town in the country.

If he had the misfortune to be injured at work, there was no Workman's Compensation Act. Certainly he could bring an action against his employer, but in the existing state of the law his chances of success were so small that he usually decided to do nothing about it.

As for the fortunate majority who were in work, hours were much longer than they are now. A man's normal working day started at six in the morning, which meant that he had to get up soon after five. (Oddly enough, in what we would now think of as a 'male chauvinist' society, it was traditionally the man's job to clear the ashes and get the kitchen fire going before he went to work).

He rarely possessed an alarm clock, and the usual arrangement was to pay a 'knocker up' threepence a week to call him at the agreed time. If he arrived after the Works whistle had stopped he was counted late, and had to lose a quarter of a day's pay. He was not allowed to start work until after the breakfast interval. He worked until half past five, with half an hour's interval for breakfast and an hour for dinner. On Saturday he finished at noon. All this adds up to a working week of fifty five and a half hours compared with the forty four or less of the present time. There were no paid holidays, and even Bank Holidays had to be 'lost'.

The cost of living was much lower than it is today of course; rent for a typical working-class house would be about four shillings a week. Fuel - a very costly item these days, was correspondingly cheaper, as were all types of consumer goods and services. In the table below, the prices of a few basic foodstuffs of comparable quality are quoted for the years 1890 and 1959.

## Prices per Pound (lb)

| Commodity | 1890 | | 1959 | |
|---|---|---|---|---|
| Butter | 1/- | *(5p)* | 4/- | *(20p)* |
| Tea | 2/- | *(10p)* | 7/- | *(35p)* |
| Oatmeal | 2½d | *(1p)* | 10d | *(4p)* |
| Sugar | 2d | *(1p)* | 8d | *(3p)* |
| Cheese | 8d | *(3½p)* | 4/- | *(20p)* |
| Bacon | 10d | *(4p)* | 5/- | *(25p)* |
| Beef | 6d - 10d | *(2½p - 4p)* | 3/- - 5/- | *(15p - 25p)* |
| Potatoes (20lb) | 8d | *(3½p)* | 5/- | *(25p)* |
| Bread (per 2lb loaf) | 2½d | *(1p)* | 11d | *(4½p)* |
| Milk (per pint) | 1½d | *(½p)* | 8½d | *(3½p)* |

These prices would indicate a present-day cost of living about four times that of 1890. It is in fact much more than that, because certain large items, notably rent and fuel, have risen disproportionately. Even so, the present basic wage is at least seven times the 1890 level with a much shorter working week leaving ample scope for overtime or some secondary occupation. Add to this the security against unemployment provided by National Insurance, and the disappearance of the dire poverty of the 'nineties is readily explained.

National Insurance covers not only unemployment, but also sickness and old age. None of this existed in 1890. By paying about sixpence a week to his Sick Club a man could make small and inadequate provision against illness, but old age was a prospect which most working people looked forward to with dread. There was no State pension. Thrifty people would have managed to save a little out of their meagre earnings, and occasionally a benevolent employer might allow a few shillings a week to an old servant. Sometimes too the man's Club would contribute up to about seven and sixpence a week, but at best the total was barely enough for decent living. In many cases the old folk had to live with their grown-up children whose burdens were already grievous enough. Failing this there was nothing left but separation and the dreaded workhouse; and going to the workhouse was looked upon as a disgrace equal to that of going to prison. Small wonder that for so many working people their whole life's economy was directed towards keeping out of it.

There were ameliorations which no longer exist today. Families were very large, so that the support of the elderly did not fall upon one or two children. Then it is a fact, strange but true, that the lower the standard of living of any given community, the more easily and naturally are the old folk absorbed into it.

A room or even a bed is shared without any feeling of deprivation on either side, and Gran helps to bring up the children without the risk of being charged with the capital crime of 'interference'.

This is just my own recollection and impression of poverty as I saw it in Runcorn towards the end of the century. The subject however was attracting the attention of social research workers in various parts of the country, and it may be of interest to give some account of their findings.

In the city of York in the year 1899, a Mr Seebohm Rowntree (a member of the Quaker family which had founded the chocolate factory) spent many months in a painstaking and detailed survey into the question of working-class poverty.

He started from a baseline he classed as 'primary poverty' - what would now be called subsistence level. This was the lowest income on which a family could maintain physical health and fitness, assuming that every penny was used to the very best advantage.

He then spent many months in a painstaking house-to-house survey to discover how families at this basic level actually spent their money, and his findings revealed amongst other things that alcohol alone accounted for six and tenpence a week. He labelled this 'secondary poverty', and his conclusion was that 28% of the poorest people lacked the necessities of life on account of the proportion of their wages which was devoted to making life endurable.

These figures applied to York in 1899, but a few years earlier, a Mr Charles Booth had made a far more extensive review of conditions in London. His methods differed somewhat from Rowntree's and London is not York, but he obtained a figure of 31% which accords well with Rowntree's 28%.

I know of no comparable investigation that was ever made in Runcorn, but it is certain that the town had its fair share of unemployment and that wages were much the same as in other parts of the country.

Yet Rowntree's findings had a special significance for Runcorn, because they produced immediate and practical results. I referred in an earlier chapter to Runcorn's 'Grand Old Man', Sir John Brunner, Managing Director of Brunner Mond and for many years MP for the Northwich Division of which Runcorn was a part. He was that 'rara avis' of the nineteenth century, an industrialist with a conscience. He studied Rowntree's findings and at once ordered that the lowest-paid of his employees should have their wages raised to a level sufficient to keep them out of the poverty ranks, assuming that they arranged their expenditure in a reasonable way.

The response was not generally as immediate as this, but the days of *laissez-faire* were numbered. Great champions were coming forward, not just from the working classes themselves but from intellectuals, and the public conscience was awakening at last to the terrible conditions under which a large section of the community existed.

The more one considers this end-of-century period, the more it assumes significance as the threshold of great social change. Not much was happening, but a great deal was about to happen. With the first trickle of scholarships, the outstanding boy from an elementary school was being given the chance of a secondary education, though many years were to pass before the trickle swelled to a flood. The thousands of physically sub-standard young men who presented themselves for medical examination in 1914 were to bring to the fore questions of malnutrition and the need for better medical and health services.

It is easy to see and tabulate the great advances the country has made in a single lifetime in promoting the physical well-being of its people; in giving them the opportunity, whatever the chances of birth and parentage, to realise the best that was in them. But it is more difficult to say with any certainty whether since 1890 we have made any corresponding moral advance, or indeed whether we have advanced at all. In attempting an answer, it would seem the obvious course to examine statistics. There would be no difficulty for instance in ascertaining the number of persons committed to prison in 1890 and comparing it with the number for 1959, but so many factors have changed that the answer would be inconclusive. Most of the offenders between the ages of fourteen and twenty-one who would formerly have been sent to prison are now dealt with in other ways, in special schools and Borstal institutions.

If we compare the average prison population of 1890 with that of 1959 we are again defeated, partly for the reason just given, and partly because prison sentences were much longer in 1890, causing the average prison population to be larger than it would otherwise have been.

If statistics do not help very much in comparing today's level of morality with that of the 'nineties, it is at any rate possible to compare some of the conditions which are likely to have a bearing on the subject. There can be little doubt for instance that the poverty and squalor of the earlier period, combined with the absence of wholesome recreation, often led to drunkenness and indirectly to such offences as wife-beating and cruelty to children.

The Methodist obsession with drink is frequently the cause of some amusement these days, but nobody not of an age to remember could have any idea of what a fearful scourge it was, two generations ago. The ruin of working-class homes was a commonplace, and the day-to-day existence of thousands of women and children must have been sheer horror. It took the magistrates in Runcorn the whole of Monday and Tuesday to deal with the weekend 'drunks', whereas now they see only a handful of cases in a year.

The situation was exacerbated by sailors from visiting ships. At that time Runcorn was a busy inland port and sailors were paid when their vessels docked, sometimes after long periods at sea. With pockets full of money they made their way along Percival Lane, and once in town were soon imbibing at the local hostelries along with bargees from the canal boats. The consequences were predictable.

To their credit the Mersey Mission to Seamen recognised the problem and in 1875 they obtained a barge which became their original facility

*William Shaw in the uniform of the Liverpool River Police, and later in front of his mission. He was the grandfather of Lily Shaw, the first 'May Queen'*

in Runcorn. The first missioner-in-charge was William Shaw. As a young man he had worked for the Liverpool River Police, and had received an award for his bravery during a hazardous rescue. His early conduct with the seafaring fraternity developed into a lifelong interest in their welfare and, largely as a result of his fund raising efforts, a site was acquired in Station Road where a small church with associated social and recreational facilities opened in 1891. He remained in this post until 1921 and, with the help of his wife, he did such outstanding work for both the sailors and the local community that the centre was always known as 'Shaw's Mission'.

Judging by the greatly reduced attendance at places of worship, one would say that influences of a directly religious character are weaker today than they used to be. On the other hand, certain other good influences are very much stronger. Young people today can find happy and healthy activity as scouts and guides and members of Youth Clubs. In the summer they can go camping, or tour the country on foot or on bicycles, staying each night at one or other of the Youth Hostels which have been set up in scores of the most beautiful localities.

In my youth there was nothing to compare with it; no organised effort at all, except by the churches, to provide young people with suitable outlets for their energy. It is hard to strike a balance between the decline in influence of the church and the emergence of these other secular organisations, but I would say that the present situation is better calculated to produce good citizens than that of two generations ago, if for one reason alone. Not everybody belonged to a church, even in 1890. Just as today, the ones who would have benefited most were the ones who stayed away. Present-day youth services can - in theory at any rate - spread a wider net.

The influence of the cinema for good or evil is difficult to assess. It was good to start with, in that it provided the first large-scale alternative to the pub as a place of entertainment, and it seemed the ideal medium for wholesome amusement which could also be educative. Unfortunately, the ideal has never been realised. Emphasis has tended more and more towards violence and horror and unsavoury sexual themes, while actors seem scarcely able to make a move without recourse to the bottle.

Radio and television have on the whole taken a more responsible attitude, and they have the added advantage of providing entertainment

*The Author as a young man, relaxing on a day out.*

within the home but it remains to be seen whether commercialisation may not win the argument here also.

If cinemas had been in existence in 1890, the seats would have had to be very cheap indeed to attract an audience. The lad just starting work counted himself lucky if he got 'sixpence for himself' out of his wages. The rest went to help support the family.

Those days have gone now and nobody would wish them back, but too much money can be as bad as too little. The youth of today has far more to spend than is good for him, with consequences well-known to all and in no need of elaboration. We have not achieved the happy mean, or we have gone beyond it, and events bring home to us the fitness of the words I heard so often quoted as a child; "Give me neither poverty nor riches, but feed me with food convenient. "

Nothing so far discussed would appear to have a decisive bearing on the undoubted change in moral standards and values. What then is the fundamental cause? There seems to be only one; the decline in home life and influence which has resulted from the changed attitude to marriage, and the changed position of women in the life of the community.

Divorce has been possible by normal process of the law since the Matrimonial Causes Act of 1857, but it was so costly and uncertain that in 1890 it was no more than a theoretical possibility for the average man. And apart from the practical obstacles, the climate of thought was against it. Religious influences were very much stronger, and the church's attitude was as uncompromising as it is today.

Volumes have been written on the pros and cons of easier divorce, but as far as the Victorians were concerned they may be simply stated. Then as now there was great hardship in a percentage of cases, the woman usually being the chief sufferer, but there was a much larger percentage of cases where difficulties were overcome because they had to be overcome. Incompatibility was a luxury which could not be afforded, and in most cases couples who were not ideally suited 'shook down' to a reasonably happy marriage. The children undoubtedly benefited in all but the most unhappy homes.

The changed position of women is a much more complex question. Already by 1890, the picture conjured up by the very phrase 'Victorian womanhood'; of downtrodden slaves on the one hand and useless young women on the other, was becoming blurred. There were still plenty of downtrodden slaves, but more ambitious girls from working and middle class homes were swelling the ranks of the pupil teachers and nurses, whose calling had been raised by Florence Nightingale to the status of an honoured profession.

Many men who had 'got on in the world' still regarded it as a measure of their material success that they could afford to keep their daughters in idleness at home with servants even to brush their hair, but more and more of these girls too were entering the professions with or without parental blessing. They didn't need the money, but some had a sense of vocation while others simply desired freedom and independence.

This attitude was more than beginning in the 'nineties; it was well under way. There was a growing sense of the need for sound education for girls, and schools which could offer it were springing up everywhere. A trickle of women were entering the Universities, and even on the athletic side, the girls were joining in! Hampered as they were by their dreadful garments, they played tennis and rode bicycles as soon as these were obtainable with two wheels of equal size. They even swam, though in bathing costumes that have been the subject of comic relief ever since.

However, except in a few localities where it was traditional, notably in the Lancashire cotton mills, very few married women worked.

In the main professions employing women; hospital nursing, teaching and the Civil Service, there was a 'marriage bar' which was not officially lifted until after the Second World War.

And had this not been the case, with so little available in the way of 'mod. cons.', running a home and bringing up a family was a full-time job. For better-to-do women and those without children the situation was rather different. They didn't need the money; but there was a wide variety of leisure interests inside and outside the home, and there was voluntary work.

Because there was such need for labour, conventions were cast aside during the Great War. Married women who were willing to work had no difficulty finding jobs, though when the war was over they remained a tiny minority until after the Second World War, when married women who continued with their jobs reached such numerical proportions as to be recognised as a separate economic force. A third of all married women in this country are now in full or part-time employment.

How can a man between seventy and eighty years of age be expected to assess dispassionately the consequences of this new element in the life of society? One appreciates the natural aspiration of the better-educated woman to a life outside the home; to an income of her own which will give her economic independence. In some cases no doubt the pooled incomes are necessary to keep the home going. But in a matter so vital to the health of the community and to its future, surely there should be some compromise. As things stand I cannot persuade myself that it is a change for the better or that women could not find an outlet for their talents without sacrificing the well-being of their children.

Perhaps I am wrong in becoming too obsessed with the figures for juvenile delinquency. They are distressing. People under twenty one are responsible for half of all the serious crime committed in this country, and juvenile crime is the cradle of all crime. But if many youngsters have misused their opportunities, many also have used them well. Borstal institutions may be full to overflowing, but so are the Technical Colleges and Universities.

It is a baffling problem, this obverse side to the new freedom and opportunity of the last forty years. Perhaps the critics are right to deplore too much 'softness' in the handling of young delinquents; there is always a tendency for the pendulum to swing dangerously far. But with all the patient effort that is being employed in trying to understand the criminal, and all the study that is being devoted to the environment and upbringing that have made him what he is, it is surely not too much to hope that the problem will be solved in the fullness of time.

# CHAPTER 14

# Changes in Thought and Outlook

The seventy years from 1890 to 1960 represent a period of greater scientific advance than any in the previous history of man. This process has been accompanied by far-reaching social and material changes which have been partly the cause and partly the result of a new way of thought. How does a man think of himself and of his neighbour, and in what way does his viewpoint differ from that of half a century ago? And how does he now think of God?

The change of attitude towards himself and his neighbour has been much more radical in the working class man than in his social superiors. Two quite contradictory elements are often to be found in the middle and upper-class make-up, though these were more marked in the last century than they are today.

The social barriers were absolute and unassailable, but the tradition of social service was equally strong and sometimes found expression under the most unlikely circumstances. A man might build up a vast fortune by dubious or even inhumane methods, and while his sacked employees were starving in their hovels his wife would be charitably engaged in carrying round the soup, with the full approval of her husband.

Jane Austen's Emma spent a proportion of her time visiting the poor in their cottages, but if Harriet Smith were so far to sink herself as to marry a prosperous farmer their friendship must be entirely at an end, as Emma herself was at pains to point out.

These two elements are not as distinct as they were, but change has been very slow and they still exist. Post-war economic circumstances have forced a new way of life upon those who two generations ago would have been well-to-do, but they cling as fiercely as ever to their traditional standard of values, and these they hand on intact to their children through example at home and sometimes by a certain type of education.

If they continue to cling to them, it may be that in the end they will perform the supreme service of 'leavening the lump'. We have still not a classless society in England and possibly we may never have it, but general prosperity and better educational opportunities have brought about much greater fluidity between one class and another, so if sufficient numbers from each generation admire and copy the best from this code of behaviour it will slowly disseminate through a much broader society.

There has been some faltering since the last war in this tradition of service. The middle and upper classes have had to accept a relatively lower standard of living. The women especially are no longer freed as in the past from day-to-day problems of existence, and there has been some feeling of resentment at the sudden rise to prosperity of large sections of the working class. This, so it appears to them, has taken place at a stroke of the Government pen and by means of confiscatory taxes on larger incomes. But tradition dies hard, and the rising generation will continue to be trained in the old principles of service to the community when armies of servants and private steam yachts have been relegated to the pages of historical novels.

The working man on the other hand has been only too pleased to break with the past; he is enjoying for the first time a sense of greatly increased importance and self-respect. Several circumstances have combined to bring this about. He is usually a member of a powerful trade union, through which he can discuss with his employer the conditions under which he shall work and the wages he shall receive. He had the vote in 1890, but he was very slow to grasp its significance; he voted for interests other than his own, so that more than thirty years were to pass before the voice of the Labour Party counted for anything in the counsels of the nation. Then the realisation came with a rush that the means of determining the way in which the country should be governed lay in the numerically superior working class.

This sense of increased importance shows itself in many ways. The working man is far more litigious than formerly - more inclined to go to law if he feels that he or some member of his family has been a victim of an injustice. This tendency has no doubt been strengthened by the fact that, provided he can put forward a prima facie case, he can secure legal assistance either free, or at a cost which takes account of his limited means.

It is not good for any man to be downtrodden; to feel he doesn't count. No doubt the new sense of importance leads him occasionally to be rather 'touchy' and to act unwisely, but that phase will pass, and in the long run he will be all the better for the feeling of self-respect that he has acquired.

And what about his attitude to his neighbour, using that term in its most comprehensive sense, to include everybody outside himself?

As the country knows to its cost, he shows extraordinary loyalty to his fellow-workmen. This is obvious from the way in which he will take action against some real or imagined injustice to one of his fellows. Conversely, his attitude towards his employers is often marked by a certain hostility and mistrust, a relic of the days when they had the power to ride roughshod over their workpeople and often did.

But while the workman of today is wonderfully loyal to his fellows he is sometimes lacking in a sense of obligation to his more remote neighbours, the 'everybody' outside his particular working group.

He may strike out of a sense of loyalty to one of his fellow workmen, but he will choose the moment to do it when he can cause maximum distress to people who have nothing whatever to do with his particular grievance and who also have their livings to make - for example by getting to work on time when the railways are at a standstill.

Edmund Burke once said: "I know not the manner of drawing up an indictment against a nation," and selfishness on the scale I have just described is by no means confined to the working man; he would quote you any number of examples from the employers who have taught him his confrontational habits. It needs the genial atmosphere of greater personal prosperity for the idea to take root and flourish that something is owing to the community, and hopefully in another generation, present methods of forcing an issue will no longer be considered an acceptable option.

Towards those who are still more remote, the coloured peoples belonging to what we knew in 1890 as The British Empire, there has been a heartening change. Our attitude then, from the humblest to the greatest in the land, was tinged with a definite element of patronage. We felt rather superior to the people we 'governed', and certainly they could not expect us to give them any say in the management of the affairs of their own country.

But the years have brought great changes. The old, comfortable sense of superiority has been shaken and this is not simply the outcome of political events but of admiration for the great natural gifts which many of these people possess. The increasing number of mixed marriages is significant, and these are by no means confined to the lower strata of society. Here is a complete volte face from even twenty or thirty years ago, when people would desperately deny insinuations of 'a streak of the tarbrush', knowing that to have it confirmed would spell social ruin.

Turning to man's attitude to God, the scientific advances of the present century have been so strongly linked in the popular mind with the decline of religious belief, that science emerges from the duel almost in the guise of Anti-Christ. What is the basis for this attitude, and how far is it justified, bearing in mind that many of our foremost scientists have lived and died convinced Christians?

Going back a very few years in time, the 'great divide' came with the new theory of evolution. It is true that by 1890 this theory was already thirty years old, but until that time it had merely been a subject for academic discussion in learned circles and had not sunk very deeply into the public consciousness. For practical purposes it may be regarded as a development of the last seventy years.

It was in 1859 that Charles Darwin wrote a book called 'The Origin of Species'. He was then fifty years of age, and had spent many years in examining various species of animals and plants, and also the fossil remains of some which were extinct. He had come to the conclusion that any given species was not the result of a sudden creation, but had developed by the slow process of evolution from a still more primitive form of life. To take a stock example familiar to most, he did not exactly believe that men were descended from monkeys, but he did come to the conclusion that man on the one hand, and the various species of apes on the other, were both descended from a common ancestor. The change was extremely gradual, taking millions of years to complete. At no stage was there a miraculous transition, but after many generations the ape-man's brain became a little larger, his head changed slightly in shape and he showed an increasing tendency to walk on two legs instead of advancing on all fours, until finally he evolved as we know him now.

According to Darwin's theory the ape-man himself was descended from some species of simpler structure, and so on back and back until all species have finally converged upon a tiny living organism, the 'amoeba', consisting of only a single cell. Many scientists believe that even this is not the beginning, but that the amoeba itself is the product of changes in lifeless, inorganic matter.

Now all this seems to differ enormously from the Biblical account of the creation of man, according to which (Gen. 2:7): 'The Lord God formed man of the dust of the ground, and breathed into his nostrils the breath of life, and man became a living soul'.

But is the difference really fundamental? The thorough-going evolutionist also believes in a process that started from 'the dust of the ground', and which through many stages finally led up to man. At some stage, he believes, the 'breath of life' became perceptible. Is it too much to say that the Biblical record is a sort of pictorial, symbolic representation of a process which really occupied long ages of time?

This theory seems easy enough for us to accept, but people today are much more conditioned to abstract thinking that the simple, trusting souls of two generations ago. For many reared in the fundamentalist belief it was the breaking point. Some, whatever their inner misgivings, clung stubbornly to the old ideas. Others abandoned them and could find nothing to put in their place. Yet a third group were able to reconcile the old teaching with the new beliefs by taking the great leap forward and seeing in the Old Testament not spiritual truth itself, but the symbols of spiritual truth.

To us it may seem simple, but to them it was tremendous. We can perhaps better understand their spiritual evolution by a parallel on a very small scale that we have all experienced. As tiny children we were happy in the belief that there was a benevolent old man called Father Christmas who came down the chimney and filled our stockings with good things. Then came disillusionment. That miraculous Father Christmas did not exist, and we no longer believed. For a time we were, so to speak, young atheists.

But for most of us there has been a further development. We have become increasingly conscious that at Christmas time there is a universal atmosphere of love and good will. People who have not been on speaking terms for months decide to 'make it up'. Men who are normally mean find themselves contributing to a fund for giving parcels to the needy. There *is* a Father Christmas, but he is something different from, and greater than, our childhood concept. No longer is he a man coming down the chimney. He is a spirit; the spirit of love and generosity filling the hearts of men and women everywhere.

It is in just this way that the fundamentalist seeker after truth suffered the destruction of his faith, to rebuild it later on foundations strengthened by the revelations of science. He began by believing every word of the Bible, in particular that in six days, God made the earth and everything therein. This God is very like a man, but much magnified. He walks in the garden and banishes Adam and Eve for their disobedience (Gen. 3:23-24). He decides that his creation of living things was a mistake and makes a fresh start with Noah and the Ark. He takes great offence because the Syrians say that although he is a God of the hills, he is not a God of the valleys. (1 Kings, 20:28). Many more illustrations might be given to show that the 'fundamentalist' God of the Bible is a being with human characteristics and frailties.

This 'human face of God' made him more understandable to the fundamentalist, but that much more difficult to reconcile with the new teachings of science. He was disillusioned, like the child unable any longer to believe in a red-robed and white-bearded Father Christmas. The old beliefs had gone, and he could find nothing to replace them. But as the child may reach a stage at which he recognises Father Christmas as a symbol of the spirit of love, so it was possible for the fundamentalist to recognise the God of the Old Testament as the symbol of a being forming the very heart of the Universe.

It is interesting to note that in the Bible itself we have this development in the concept of God - the realisation that He is greater than had previously been thought. Jacob shared the belief which was common in primitive times that God belonged strictly to his own locality. When he was compelled to leave home, he was saddened not so much by leaving the place itself, as by leaving his God behind. Night came, and he settled down to rest. It was useless to pray, because in this place far from his house there was no God to hear him. He went to sleep and dreamed of a ladder on which the angels of God were ascending and descending, and he awoke with a new and enlarged concept. The God he worshipped when he was at home was here too! "Surely the Lord is in this place and I knew it not!"

And so the men of 'yesterday', travelling from the familiar spiritual home to one in which ideas of evolution held sway, felt sadly enough at first that they had left God behind. Later, there came to many of them the conviction that had come to Jacob.

But there are many no doubt of the present age as well as those of my childhood, who have journeyed into what seems to them the godless wilderness of science. For them there is no vision of the angels. Is there then no common ground on which they can meet those who have seen the ladder that joins earth to heaven?

Surely yes - the common ground of the Good Life. Whether a man has seen the vision or not, he may still feel the high call to forgive his enemies, to pour oil and wine into the wounds of the traveller who has fallen by the way. He may still accept the teaching that true greatness lies in service: teaching conveyed by that great parable in action, the Washing of the Feet. He is free to join the ranks of those who, though unable to say "Lord, Lord," may yet do the will of the Father which is in Heaven.

*Mother in old age.*

# EPILOGUE

It was a reversal of the usual trend, in that five of the eight children who died in infancy were girls, and the three sisters who survived were a tragic trio.

In 1898, Nellie was the victim of a serious road accident. It was Camden's Sunday school Treat, a wagonette outing to Helsby Hill, and Nellie as the class teacher had a coveted seat on the box beside the driver. The horses took fright when a passing cyclist rang his bell, and bolted. Unable to negotiate a double bend where a bridge crossed both the canal and a road running beside it, they crashed over the parapet, and fell thirty feet into the street below, taking the wagonette with them. The children inside had some protection, but Nellie was thrown wide and her head dashed against the bridge abutment. There were no x-rays of course, but she was bleeding from the ears and may well have fractured the base of her skull. After lying unconscious for three weeks she appeared to make a miraculous recovery, but her hearing started to fail and within a very short time she was stone deaf. It was a sad postscript to her story that if the accident had happened fifty or sixty years later her hearing could have been restored with a fenestration operation.

Bessie went blind in her mid-thirties, and there was no diagnosis beyond the fact that it was due to atrophy of the optic nerve. After her death at the age of seventy eight, a post mortem revealed that she had a large brain tumour. It was non malignant, but could not have been removed with the surgical techniques available at that time.

Their tragedies were mitigated to some extent by their unfailing cheerfulness, their determination to live as normal lives as possible and their care for, and interest in their families.

Bertha's story was perhaps the saddest of all. She never married, but continued to live with her widowed mother and nursed her devotedly through three years of a painful illness which ended with her death in 1927. Bertha was never able to remake her life, and died of pneumonia when she was only forty seven. Antibiotics were still a decade away, but maybe she could have survived if she had felt it was worth the struggle.

Of the five sons, William and Walter did inherit something of their father's business ability, as did Sam when acting independently. He and George successfully expanded the insurance connection which their father had built up, but this was only their bread and butter. Their real interest lay in much more exciting - and hopefully lucrative - ventures.

George's outstanding gift was as a communicator. At one time, on Friday nights, he ran a series of open-air religious meetings in Devonshire Square, and he was just as successful in persuading his hearers to seek salvation as he was at selling them insurance policies. Unfortunately, more than one business venture foundered, not through lack of effort and commitment, but through lack of judgement, and shortly after the First World War he and Sam emigrated to Canada with their families. They set up in a real estate business, this time with Sam at the helm, and though it wasn't the Klondike Goldrush they made a reasonable living.

George, never satisfied with the predictable, occupied his spare time and energy inventing a machine guaranteed to confer good health and longevity on its regular users. He was engaged on a new and improved model when he died at eighty one. The curious thing was that when he operated it himself it seemed to produce results, and Walter always believed he had natural healing powers.

George and Sam were the eldest of the surviving sons, William and Walter the youngest, with Charlie on his own in between. He had the misfortune to lose all his savings in a bank crash, and this may have led to his achieving the well nigh impossible feat of going bankrupt in a Lancashire fish and chip shop. As a result of this double disaster he wisely decided that Free Enterprise was not for him, and for the rest of his working life he had a clerical job in an import and export business in Manchester.

The family's natural optimism reached its apogee in Charlie. Nobody better deserved the associated adjective 'cheerful'. He did some local preaching and firmly believed that the Christian message should be one of joy. Hearing on one occasion that a neighbour was in a state of deep depression, he called in to see what he could do to cheer her. "What about a few verses from 'We happy band of brothers' Mrs Murphy?" he suggested. He embarked with gusto on Verse One, and it did at least rouse the patient from her apathy, because she looked up at him with a pleading eye and said "Please don't, Charlie!"

The ties of their early youth held William and Walter together to the end of their lives, and they died within a few months of each other, yet they were so very different. The moral standards held firm, but William was the only member of the family to reject the faith he had been brought up in. He was not a happy man. He had a good job in the Civil Service, but failed to achieve the promotion he had hoped for, and reacted to this with a bitterness which cast a shadow over the rest of his life. Perhaps Walter had him in mind when he refers in the book to those who can't accept a 'No' from life.

Nobody was better acquainted with life's 'Noes' than Walter. It had been his dearest ambition to be a doctor, but for a poor boy at the turn of the century it was a pipe dream. The cost of the training would have been prohibitive, and his family were unaware that expert advice was available on special funding arrangements for promising students.

As previously mentioned he was awarded a scholarship and attended the Verdin Grammar School, Winsford, where he was a pupil for four years. He kept himself from the age of sixteen, teaching in the day and studying at night in an attempt to gain a science degree by means of a correspondence course. Finding that this was not practicable, he borrowed the money from Sam, for whom he always had a special affection, and with this loan he supplemented a teacher training grant at what was then University College, Nottingham, so obtaining a degree in chemistry.

Returning to teaching it was a not unreasonable hope that he might achieve a 'Headship', and with that end in view he took an Honours degree in modern languages, studying for it in his spare time with a correspondence course. He also achieved the F. C. P., the highest teaching diploma then available. But here again he found the way blocked because he had not been to a prestigious University. Ideally Oxford and a degree in Classics were needed to get you there; even a 'Third' would do.

So it was that he started his writing career, finding in the process modest fame and fortune, and self-fulfilment.

After such a prolific start the family of William and Sarah is now extinct in Runcorn. Three further generations have scattered far and wide with varying fortunes, but all can trace their beginnings to the day when Father made his dramatic descent from the top of the garden gate and Mother happened to pop her head over the wall.